MW00655461

LEARNING DISABILITIES: THERE IS A CURE

A Guide for Parents, Educators and Physicians

Revised and Expanded Second Edition

With

Two new chapters:

Learning a Foreign Language
The Best Mathematics Approach

Addie Cusimano, M.Ed.

Learning Disabilities: There is a Cure
A Guide for Parents, Educators and Physicians
Revised and Expanded Second Edition:
Copyright © 2010 by Addie Cusimano

Published by:
ACHIEVE PUBLICATIONS
Lansdale, Pennsylvania
USA
http://www.achievepublications.com

First Edition Copyright © 2001
ISBN 0-615-12053-9

Revised and Expanded Second Edition:
ISBN 978-0-972-77627-1

Library of Congress Control Number 2009909014

*This book is dedicated to my mother and father
who instilled in me a wonderful appreciation of education
and the desire to help my fellow man.*

A special thank you
to my husband, daughter and son
for their patience and support
with all of my educational endeavors.

CONTENTS

PREFACE

AUTHOR'S PERSONAL STORY

As I stood nervously in front of my third grade class on my first day of teaching, I never imagined that someday I would be delving deeply into the reading problems of children, working closely with learning disabled children, and finding so many answers.

My first year of teaching was like a dream come true. From my own first day of kindergarten, I had felt such admiration for teachers, those people who were so knowledgeable and so willing to impart their knowledge to others. I dreamed that some day, I too, would teach. And now, I really was a teacher! I remember thinking during my first year of teaching that it was incredible that I should be getting paid for doing something that was so much fun! My third graders were eager to learn and very cooperative. However, I was perplexed as to why some could read well and others were so far behind. After all, I was following the manual and teaching them all the same way. What was wrong?

When my daughter was born, I decided to stay at home with her, which was customary in those days. I accepted a request by a neighbor to tutor her son, Christopher, who could barely read. It wasn't until then that I began to closely observe the individual facets of reading problems. It was an inspiration for me to hear his mother tell me how Christopher would run home from school and excitedly say, "I have to go to Mrs. Cusimano's house." Not only was Christopher reading better and doing better in school, but also Christopher's mother was amazed at how much happier he was, and how much confidence he was beginning to express in his ability to read and perform in school! The joy I felt from knowing that I was making such an impact in this child's life gave me more satisfaction than I had ever experienced. I was hooked! This was what I wanted to do with my life, devote it to children with reading problems.

As word got around of Christopher's improvement in reading, I soon had my hours filled to the brim with students in need of help. As new reading problems surfaced, I did more and more independent research into reading problems and the solutions available for teachers. I read every journal and current text on the teaching of reading that I could find. I began to administer diagnostic tests to determine the weaknesses and strengths of my students before I began the remediation. This led to even faster remediation since I could pinpoint the weak skills more quickly than the random manner of just waiting until weaknesses surfaced. It did not take me long to realize that no single test on the market would give me all the answers I needed, and so I began to pick and choose various subtests from several tests to find what I needed. I also determined that there was not one student who responded well enough to just one remedial approach. I needed to combine several approaches to get the results I wanted. It all became very clear to me that reading and learning were made up of various facets, all of which needed to be well developed in order for a child to be able to read and learn with ease.

Two friends encouraged me, a principal and a reading specialist who kept saying to me, "You have such a wonderful understanding of problem readers. You should get your reading specialist certification so that you can work in our school to help us." I decided to go back to college. The course work was very easy for me since I already had first-hand experience with so many children and was familiar with most of the concepts and materials presented. For this reason, I had a straight A record in graduate school and, finally, my master's degree, reading specialist certificate and provisional state certification to prove it!

I then acquired a reading teacher position at a middle school. While I enjoyed the work very much, I found myself becoming very frustrated. I worked with children from fourth through eighth grade. My largest class numbered thirteen students. My smallest class consisted of six children who came to me twice a week for forty-minute sessions. Even with my smallest class, there just wasn't enough time to give my students the individual attention they deserved. Although they were in the same grade, these children had varied needs and were at different instructional levels. I felt it would be best not to teach them as a class, for some children in the class would already know what I was teaching and others may not yet be ready for that level of instruction. What to do?

I realized that the best I could do for each student

during the short period of time available was to individualize the program for each child. I did this by finding materials that were at the instructional level of each child, setting up an individualized instructional plan, and then remediating intensely, moving from one child to another during the class period. Some small group instruction was done to try to develop the learning or basic phonetic skills for which all of these children were in such great need. But on many days, if I could give each child five minutes of one to one instruction I was lucky. Time was the factor. There never was enough time!

At the end of the first year, my students made, on average, a one and a half-year gain. But I was discouraged. Many of these children had been two, to two and a half years behind in reading, and while they had advanced during the school year, they were far behind in reading for their next grade. How would they ever catch up and reach their grade level in reading? Although I was discouraged, the reading coordinator told me that the gains that my students made were *greater* than any reading specialist had ever accomplished at their school, and that I should be proud of their successes. But I wasn't. I felt sad. No wonder there were so many children always lagging behind in reading. For the most part, they were not slow learners, but children with average to above average intelligence. Something was wrong here!

I started to gather statistics on my severely learning disabled students, students with average to above average IQ's with serious learning skill deficiencies. I made an appointment to see the superintendent to explain to him that I needed to have these children, in particular, for a longer period of time during the week, preferably one-hour a day every day of the week. He listened politely, agreed with me that a longer time was needed, but explained that there wasn't enough money available, for in order to do this an additional reading teacher would have to be hired.

Frustrated and discouraged that there was no way in this public school district that I could ever meet the needs of all of my students, I began to mentally design a program that I thought would work. I was convinced at that time that individualized and one to one instruction was the only way that I could give perfectly intelligent, learning disabled children what they needed and deserved to bring them up to grade level and above in reading. As soon as I acquired my permanent state certification, I resigned to open my own learning center.

On September 14, 1978 as I walked from the courthouse with an official document in hand saying that I was the owner of my own school, I felt a feeling of exuberance. I was now free to set up a learning center in a manner that I knew would be the most helpful for children. Now I could pursue my desire, for what I sincerely felt was God's plan for me, to help children in need.

A few months later, my hours all booked, I hired my first teacher. I was very concerned about her being able to teach the way I taught, continuing with an ongoing diagnosis of her students as she taught, and getting the results I wanted. So I set up a special training session, and kept apprised of her program through her lesson plans, observation and discussion of each of her student's work. Her students were progressing nicely! I was pleased.

As word spread of the success of the students at my learning center, primarily by word of mouth of happy parents, my school grew. Within three years I had five teachers working for me. I was delighted that now I could help so many more students! It was very exciting to watch the growth of these students, and rewarding to hear parents express their appreciation of the positive changes in their children.

For seventeen years I continued my research on learning disabled children, and offered specialized programs for children who ranged from slow learners to gifted. My program for learning disabled children encompassed all of their learning needs. My elementary program for gifted students offered foreign language development as well as diversified enrichment activities far beyond a basic school curriculum. Through the years, the reputation of my school grew to the point where I continuously had referrals by physicians and educators throughout the area, especially neurologists and psychologists who often dealt with children who were learning disabled. The results at my learning center were impressive to parents as well as professionals. In the course of a few years, I had more than twenty-five teachers and over one hundred and twenty-five students!

The gains that the students at my learning center made were astonishing. The average child made a two, to two and a half years' gain in a year in reading. I had many severely learning disabled students who came to me as "non-readers" in third or fourth grade who not only overcame their disability but, also, went on to college without having to struggle at all. One learning disabled student became a lawyer, one earned a master's degree in forensic science, and another became a minister. All of our learning disabled students graduated from high school and many went to college.

Almost every day we read in the newspaper or hear on television reports of weaknesses, and gains, in our educational system. For some time, parents, and educators, have been deeply concerned about the number of students with reading difficulties in our public schools. For many years statistical reports have stated that two out of every ten children in the United States were diagnosed as learning disabled. In 1994 the *Department of Education* reported that forty percent of all fourth graders in the United States were reading below the basic reading level. As a result of serious concerns about the performance level of our students, a *National Reading Panel* was formed and the *No Child Left Behind Act* of 2001 was enacted. While improvements have been seen in the overall reading level of students since the enactment, with nine year olds obtaining the best scores in reading since 1971, we still have a long way to go.

Approximately 2.7 million public school students have been diagnosed as learning disabled, causing some local governments to express a concern that the *No Child Left Behind Act* has not provided an adequate oversight of special education. The *Alliance for Excellent Education* reported in 2009 that 1.2 million students in the United States do not graduate from high school. In some inner city public high schools, the dropout rate is as high as fifty percent, with twenty-five percent of these students classified as learning disabled.

While we are beginning to make progress, continued efforts need to be done to improve the quality of education in the United States with much more attention being given to inner city school students and children with special needs.

After working intensively for more than forty years with learning disabled students as well as those who were not, I am convinced that the same skill development and teaching techniques that worked with students at my school should be implemented throughout the nation in our elementary curriculum. In this way, all children, from learning disabled to gifted, would be provided with the skills they need to reach their full learning potential and achieve academic success.

A few years ago I left my thriving learning center and took early retirement, not because I thought my work was done, but because I decided that I wanted to live near my children and grandchildren. This necessitated a major move. I gave up my work with the belief, however, that I could help even more students by writing a book that would help parents, educators, and physicians to better understand the scope of deficiencies that children, and in particular learning disabled children, face. There *are* solutions to these problems. For, we *can* greatly improve the overall performance level of all students if we use the right approach.

Addie Cusimano
April 2002
Revised 2010

CHAPTER 1

MISCONCEPTIONS OF LEARNING DISABILITIES

Parents, and even educators, are often confused about what it means when their child or student is learning disabled. The term "disabled" leads too many people to believe that a learning disabled child is innately a slow learner or retarded and that there is little or no hope for a cure. Nothing could be farther from the truth! The term needs to be changed to more closely reflect its true meaning. A more accurate description of the child would be "learning deficient." But, in the meantime, I will continue to use the term "learning disabled" in order not to cause any confusion.

A learning disabled child is one who innately has an *average* to *superior* IQ (intelligence quotient), and serious learning skill deficiencies. The learning skills are visual perception, visual memory, auditory perception and auditory memory. Deficiencies in these areas will severely hinder a student's growth in the basic subjects of mathematics, English (including written expression), history, science, reading and spelling. They will also interfere with a child's thinking, study and work skill development. As a result, a severely learning disabled child's overall performance level will often be two, to two and a half years below his actual grade level.

The term "dyslexic" is sometimes misunderstood in its relationship to "learning disabled." Dyslexic is a specific term used to describe a learning disabled child whose skills are hindered in the language areas only, that is, in the areas of reading, spelling, English (including written expression), mathematics word problems, history, and science. In other words, a dyslexic child, that is a child with dyslexia, will not experience serious difficulties in the calculation of mathematics. Therefore, the terms, learning disabled or dyslexic child can be used interchangeably whenever the language areas *only* are affected and mathematical calculation does not enter the picture.

To many people, the term dyslexia has become synonymous with reversals of letters in writing, reading and spelling. Sometimes, parents, and even some educators, become concerned that a child might be dyslexic when they see the child reversing letters while reading or spelling. If a beginning reader has not internalized the left-right directionality of letters in words, he often will reverse them when writing. It is not necessarily an indication that the child is dyslexic. He often just needs time and practice to develop an automatic internalization of the direction of letters. On the other hand, by the time the child is at the mid to end of first grade and beyond, reversals may be an indication that a child is dyslexic. It is very important to understand, however, that a dyslexic child has a multitude of deficiencies and that a problem with reversals is only one small facet of the disability. When signs of reversals are still evident by the middle of first grade, and the student is experiencing a great deal of difficulty learning to read, a thorough diagnostic evaluation is in order. This evaluation should examine all facets of learning skills and not just address the problems of reversals.

There is a common belief that students who are diagnosed as learning disabled can be helped somewhat, but that they will always be learning disabled. This is not true. Throughout my years of working with learning disabled students, I have seen many students completely overcome their disability. Some of these students entered my learning center when they were in fourth grade, barely able to read. These children could only read three or four words, and would be classified by most professionals as "non-readers." In all cases these children were severely learning disabled. Once a program was initiated to develop their learning and basic reading skills, these children made astonishing gains in reading. All of these "non-readers" were reading at the second half of second grade or first half of third grade level with only one year of remediation.

Billy came to me at the second half of sixth grade. He had serious learning skill deficiencies and was reading two and a half years below his present grade level. After a thorough diagnosis was made, an individualized program was designed to help Billy develop his basic reading, writing, and learning skills. Emphasis was placed on the development of his visual perception, auditory memory and visual memory skills. Billy's self-image, like that of so many severely learning disabled students, was very poor. He would walk into the learning center with his head down, and would not talk to anyone while he waited to meet with his teacher. After a few months, however, Billy's reading and learning skills began to develop to the point where he was reading at a second half of fifth grade level. This was astonishing to his parents, who had tried many avenues of remediation that had failed to help their son learn to read. Billy was now walking into the learning center with his head held high. He was beginning to become more and more talkative and personable.

By the time Billy was in eighth grade, he was not only reading at grade level but had overcome his disabilities. Billy continued to come to the learning center from time to time for instruction in study skills or support with various courses until he graduated from high school. After graduation from high school, Billy was accepted into a local community college. His parents reported that he did well. He subsequently went on to a four-year college and earned a Bachelor of Science degree.

I would occasionally hear from Billy's parents about the status of their son's life, but I hadn't seen Billy to talk to him. One day, much to my delight, a tall, young man walked into my office, shook my hand and said, "Remember me? I'm Billy S., Mrs. Cusimano. I wanted to come to thank you again, and to tell you and my teacher that I have just received an academic scholarship to continue my education in forensic studies at Northeastern University. I want you to know that I still have all of my flashcards from my first years here at the Center. I'm saving them so that someday I can show my own children how I overcame the greatest hurdle in my life. If they ever have a problem in their lives, they will know that no matter how great it is, they can overcome it." The flashcards were a symbol for him of his perseverance and accomplishment. While I have had a multitude of touching thank you notes from students and parents over the years, I think that this personal thank you from Billy was the greatest of them all!

My philosophy has always been that encouragement and praise begets greater achievement. Therefore, at my learning center, the teachers were required to use a very positive approach when working with their students. There was no negativism whatsoever. The more positive teachers are with children, the greater the gains. Students, especially learning disabled students who often have a poor self-image, tend to become anxious and make more errors if they are corrected in a negative manner. Praise and encouragement helps them to relax, and thus allows them to be more alert during the learning process.

With the right type of remediation and the elimination of learning skill deficiencies, learning disabled children can function in the academic world as well as students who have never had to struggle with disabilities. I have seen many students, not only overcome their disability but, also, go on to college and graduate school to become lawyers, teachers and scientists, graduating with honors. The secret lies in identifying, and then developing the weak learning skills while systematically developing basic skills.

It is a fact that many learning disabled students have a high IQ. They certainly have the innate potential to go on to college, undergraduate and even graduate school. But should they enter college with serious learning skill deficiencies? I say emphatically, "No!" There is a widespread belief today that we cannot remediate some learning disabled students, even those who are innately intelligent enough to go to college. Therefore, it is thought that we must accept these young people, disabilities and all, into our colleges, offer extra programs to guide them through college, and ask their professors to make special exceptions for them. It is my feeling that there should not be any students in college with learning disabilities. We can, and should, erase the disabilities of college bound students *before* they enter college.

I have had numerous calls from college professors, frustrated by the fact that they do not know how to work with learning disabled students in their classes, asking me to advise them on how to assist their students. I remember one professor calling to ask if he should give his learning disabled students a copy of his test ahead of time to take home so that they could prepare their answers before the test day. While I know clearly the problems that learning disabled students face in college, I feel that a total injustice occurs when we give learning disabled students an unfair advantage. The injustice is certainly in the unfairness to the rest of the class, but most importantly, to the learning disabled students. I feel that we have over-compensated for learning disabled students to the point of hurting them.

All too often I hear professionals talking about learning disabled students "learning to compensate" for their disability. The truth is that it is not the learning disabled students who have learned to compensate for their disability, but rather the professionals who have made compensations for the learning disabled students. Instead of having students face their problems, giving them the techniques that they need to learn to overcome their disability, professionals sometimes offer alternatives that not only make them feel different from other students but are impractical. Often we hear of recommendations for students who experience difficulties with handwriting, for example, to learn to type. First, these students have to learn to type at least as rapidly as their fellow classmates write by hand. That can be very time consuming and frustrating, especially for elementary students who are often the ones who are advised to type their work. Secondly, typing is applicable primarily for composition writing assignments, not for everyday work in school where workbooks and worksheets are used. In addition, recommendations are sometimes made for test questions to be read to learning disabled students or to have them take tests on a computer in an effort to make test taking easier for the students. In some cases these students are taken out of class to take their tests, at a time when they should be in class and not missing out on the teaching of new skills. Other exceptions are made for learning disabled students such as allowing them to have extra time for homework assignments or report writing. Psychologically, it can do more harm than good to treat students with learning disabilities differently from other classmates. It often embarrasses the learning deficient students and does nothing to improve their already low self-image. But, most importantly, this does not solve the problem. It only gives students a crutch, a sense that they need others to make special exceptions for them, a sense that they are not as intelligent as other children are, and, in some cases, a sense of hopelessness.

Should educators give learning disabled students a longer period of time to take tests? We do this all the time, even with the SAT college entrance examinations. When students are in elementary school, and teachers are just beginning to help students to overcome their disabilities, allowing a reasonable amount of extra time for youngsters to complete their work or tests is understandable. I am a strong believer, however, that learning skill deficiencies should be eliminated in elementary school *before* students enter junior high school, thereby leaving the consideration of extra time needless.

The fact that special compensations presently have to be made at the college level for learning disabled students is a serious concern. We must think about how these learning disabled students will function in the work force after graduation, if they have had compensation after compensation made for them while they were in high school or college. Most bosses will not say to an employee, "Well, Bill, I really need this work done by 3 p.m. today, but because you're learning disabled, I'll give you until tomorrow morning." How many owners of companies or supervisors can afford to overlook frequent spelling errors, lack of clarity and slowness in completion of, let's say, an engineering proposal that is going to a company for a multimillion dollar job? When the learning disability drastically hinders the effectiveness of the employee, employers certainly do not want that person in their company. We need to be realistic. Therefore, we must eliminate the problems that face learning-disabled students, and it must be done in elementary school in order to give these intelligent youngsters an equal and just opportunity to enter college and to confront the work force on an equal plane with others.

It is important to point out also that if serious learning and basic skill deficiency problems are not addressed properly and eliminated at the elementary level, they become compounded at the middle or junior high school and high school levels. As these students advance in grades there is a vast amount of academic information that they simply *cannot* grasp, and as a result, they often are no longer able to perform at their innate potential level. Learning disabled students, whose IQ scores are in the "average" to "above average" range when they are in elementary school, sometimes score in the "low average" range when they are in high school. This happens, not because their innate potential has lessened, but because their learning skill deficiencies have hindered their learning for so many years that their innate potential, once they are in high school, is masked by their deficiencies. *Learning disabilities, therefore, must be addressed and erased at the elementary level.*

There are four major learning skills that are at the root of learning disabilities. They are visual perception, visual memory, auditory perception and auditory memory. They are not complex. And, when the right kind of remediation is given on a consistent basis, these learning skill deficiencies can be erased. If remediation of these skills is coupled with a systematic development of basic subjects as well as a strong thinking, work and study skills program, learning disabilities disappear.

If all elementary school curriculums were to include work in all of the learning skill areas for all students, severe learning disabilities would, most likely, be almost non-existent in our schools. For those few children who may still experience some weaknesses in the learning skill areas, more concentrated attention to the development of these skills would easily erase the weaknesses. It can be done! Learning disabilities can be prevented and cured!

CHAPTER 2

CLARIFYING VISUAL PERCEPTION

Before beginning a discussion of visual perception, it is essential to address the issue of vision, meaning *visual acuity*. The term *visual acuity* refers to a child's eyesight and how clearly a child sees with his eyes. Every child, but especially one with visual perception problems, should be given an eye screening test by the school nurse for distant and near point vision. When a visual screening report indicates that a child's vision is 20/20, it means that at a distance of twenty feet that child's vision is as good as the average person's vision at twenty feet. This would indicate, for example, that the child has good vision for reading material written on the chalkboard from his desk seat at a distance of twenty feet. It does not mean that he necessarily has good vision for close work such as reading from a book that he is holding.

Years ago, I worked with a little girl, named Katy, a second grader who was experiencing difficulty with reading. I noticed that she would squint, and that her eyes would become watery whenever she tried to read from her basal reader. I suspected a vision problem and asked her mother, who was a nurse, to have Katy's eyes examined by a physician. She did. The doctor's diagnosis was that Katy's vision was fine and that she did not need eyeglasses. I accepted the diagnosis with reservation and confusion. If her eyes were fine, why were they watering? I continued to work with Katy, keeping an on-going observation of her eyes. I noticed that when she read from the chalkboard or from books with large print, her eyes appeared normal. However, when she was asked to read from a book with small print, she would squint and her eyes would begin to water. One day I noticed that her eyes were watering to the point that drops were actually rolling down her cheek. "That's it!" I thought, "I am going to ask her mother to take her to another doctor for a second opinion."

A few weeks later Katy walked into class with eyeglasses, a big smile on her face and a bookmark in her hand. She said, "Look, Mrs. Cusimano. I can *even* read this bookmark!" I looked at the tiny print on the bookmark and smiled. Katy never had watery eyes again, and without eyestrain was able to move along very quickly with her reading remediation.

Although Katy had been given a screening at school to check her vision prior to the doctor's examination, that screening was only for distant vision. She had been asked to read a Snellen wall chart which is placed at a distance of twenty feet from the student. No screening had been done for near point vision.

In order to screen for near point vision, a child's vision must be checked with a chart containing small print which is placed at a distance of thirteen to sixteen *inches* away from the child's eyes, depending on the chart used. Unfortunately, not all school districts are equipped to screen children for near point vision. Yet, this is an essential prerequisite for reading. If there is a problem with eye strain, blurred vision or a problem with shifting the eyes along the lines of print in a book quickly and accurately, these problems will interfere tremendously with the ease at which a child learns to read. Educators need to look for signs from a student that may be an indicator of a near point visual acuity problem. These would include squinting, watering eyes, eye rubbing, covering one eye when reading, or glancing away frequently while reading material that is at a close proximity to the child. All children should be screened in school for distant and near point vision difficulties, beginning in kindergarten. In addition, parents should be encouraged to have their child's eyes examined by an eye doctor who is a child vision specialist. A child vision specialist is a doctor who has had special training to examine a child's eye-teaming (how the two eyes work together), focusing, eye movement (how the eyes shift from one point to another), as well as distant and near point visual acuity.

While good visual acuity is a prerequisite for good visual perception, they are not one and the same. A child can have good visual acuity and still have a serious visual perception weakness because visual acuity involves how we actually *see* words, while visual perception has to do with how we *perceive* words.

One of the four major learning skill areas is visual perception. Visual perception involves being able to note likenesses and differences, especially differences, in pictures, letters, numbers, and finally, and most importantly, words. It is an essential skill for students to develop for all core subject learning. It begins to develop naturally with most children when they are preschoolers. However, there are those children who, while they may be exposed to visual perceptual preschool materials, do not develop this skill automatically as preschoolers, and, therefore, need formal instruction for its development. In addition, all children need to have more advanced visual perception skills presented to them on a developmental basis once they enter kindergarten.

Children with visual perception problems will often reverse numbers, letters and words. B's and d's are reversed as well as p's and q's, 2's and 3's, and words like *was* and *saw*. Some educators speak of this as "mirror imagery" which leads people to interpret the problem of visual perception as being one in which children actually see letters or words in reverse. At one time a national organization for learning disabled children was actually televising an advertisement showing words on the screen with the letters reversed, insinuating that learning disabled children see words in reverse. Nothing could have been more misleading, or farther from the truth. These reversals are not made because children see a letter, number or word backwards, but because their perception of the item is either in reverse or not completely accurate. When children read *saw* for *was*, they often do so because they have not internalized the left-right directionality of words. Their eye movement is often in reverse or erratic and, therefore, they read the word as *saw* instead of *was*. If you ask those same children to spell the word for you, they will often spell the word correctly. They will spell it as *w a s*. Therefore, it is apparent that these children are not seeing the word in reverse, but rather perceiving it inaccurately. This appears to be due to the fact that they have not internalized the left-right movement of the eye for reading. Often when these same children are asked to read the word a second time, they will read the word correctly. They will read *was* as *was*. Or they may spell it correctly, *w a s*, and yet read it as *saw*. This is because, while children physically see the word correctly, their mental processing of the word may be in reverse. They have not internalized reading from left to right. The reason they sometimes read it correctly on the second try is because they correct their directionality. However, because their left-right eye movement is not automatic, later on, even in the same story or paragraph, they may reverse the same word again.

Visual perception problems are not solely exhibited by complete reversals of letters, numbers or words. Many students with visual perception problems will display inaccuracies in their reading that are not exact reversals of the whole word. For example, they may read *brake* as *bake*, *danced* as *dance*, *anticipated* as *anticipate*, and *historical* as *historic*. These students frequently omit letters in their reading, and thus do not perceive the entire word accurately. Others will add letters that are not there as they read, reading *skipping for skip, drove* for *dove, graduated* for *graduate,* and *reinstitute* for *institute*. Remember, it is not that they see the word inaccurately, but rather that they perceive it incorrectly.

Another way in which students with visual perception problems will display this weakness is with substitution. They will sometimes read, *buggy* as *carriage, mother* as *mom*, *grandfather* as *grandpa*. In these instances, students silently read the word accurately, but in the process of sending the message to the brain and then stating what they have read, there is a substitution. The word is taken in with a perceptual correctness but is not processed in the mind in the same pattern that it is taken in and, therefore, is expressed inaccurately. This type of visual perception problem is not as common as that of reversals, omissions, and additions in reading. Not all students with visual perception problems will exhibit substitution in their reading. Most students, however, will exhibit reversals, additions and omissions.

Along with the problem of not having established an automatic left-right eye movement in his reading, a student with a visual perception problem does not focus on the details of words and frequently is unaware of the differences in words that are similar in appearance. Words such as *this* and *that, when* and *then, where* and *there, and* and *an, my* and *by, how* and *now, where* and *were* often cause problems for beginning readers. It becomes frustrating for the child, and even more frustrating for the teacher or parent, when the child is told the correct word over and over again and still reads it incorrectly. The problem lies in the fact that a young child, especially a beginning reader and even one who is not learning disabled, often does not note differences in similar words.

Learning disabled students who have not been remediated properly by the end of first grade will carry this weakness with them to second grade. As they advance in school, if they do not receive concentrated remediation, their perceptual inaccuracies often become more and more noticeable and will begin to interfere more and more with their reading comprehension and their accuracy in all subject areas. This poses a situation of great frustration, not only for the students, but also for everyone who works with the students.

Sometimes frustrated parents, and even some teachers, are unintentionally insensitive in working with a beginning reader. They will often say to the youngster, "Look at the word. You're not looking at it!" or "I just told you that word. I'm not telling it to you again!" These comments tend to make the child anxious about reading and the youngster then begins to make even more errors. Therefore, it must be stressed that patience, kindness and understanding must be displayed at all times. Asking a child to look more carefully at a word, calmly, and with a patient tone of voice, may assist a beginning reader without a visual perception problem to read more accurately. However, saying this to a child with a visual perception problem is often futile, for the child simply may not be able on his own to accurately perceive differences in similar words. Therefore, it is essential for all who work with the child to point out and work with the child on the differences of these words. The two similar words should be presented to the child side by side. Differences should be pointed out, and consistent and repeated practice in reading the two similar words should be a part of his program. It is also very helpful to have the child spell one of the words, saying the word after he spells it. This should be repeated several times. Then the same process should be done with the similar word. At this point, if the child continues to confuse these words, the child should be asked to trace one of the words, spell it as he traces it and then read the word orally. Then, the other similar word should be handled in the same manner. The purpose is to help the child to note and internalize the differences in the words so that, in time, it becomes automatic for him to focus on differences in words. It works!

A very effective way to help a student internalize the difference between similar words is to have him trace each letter of the word while spelling it orally and then read the word orally. It is especially effective if the procedure is repeated over and over again until the child feels that he *really* knows the word. This technique is called the VAKT technique. The initials stand for visual, auditory, kinesthetic and tactile. By using all of these senses the child internalizes each word, thus forming a permanent connection in his mind of the word. This approach is particularly effective for parents and teachers to use when two similar words are constantly confused by the child and pointing out the differences or practicing reading them has not helped. The VAKT technique is also a valuable tool to use with a student who has a problem with number reversals. Asking the child to trace the numbers, saying them as he traces, helps him to internalize the correct directionality and formation of the numbers.

A question that often arises is, "Should a parent or teacher interrupt a child while he is reading to correct frequent minor inaccuracies?" Some educators feel that ignoring them is better because, if the student is stopped frequently while he is reading, he will miss the comprehension of the sentence. They are also concerned about the student being frustrated and developing a poor self-image. Some educators feel that those *little* words are not important anyway for, after all, what difference does it make if a child says, *an* for *and*? They feel it doesn't seriously affect the sentence sense anyway. I disagree. It has been my experience that, while a student's comprehension may be hindered somewhat in the process of rereading a word, more good is accomplished than harm. Those minor inaccuracies often change the meaning of the sentence so drastically that ignoring the inaccuracy only adds to the misinterpretation of meaning. For example, if a student reads the sentence, "This little dog likes us." as "His little bog look as," he simply cannot decipher the meaning accurately. By interrupting the student, we are focusing on the visual perception problem when it happens, the essential time to correct it. It makes the student aware of what he is doing, and when the student rereads the word, this time correctly, his comprehension of the sentence is more accurate. While educators should never work at the frustration level of a child, there are many students who can be stopped frequently and, with a gentle and kind approach, be asked to look once again at the word that was incorrectly read without becoming frustrated. This helps a student to feel that each word is significant. It helps him to internalize the feeling of how one must focus carefully on each word, and that every word is important to the meaning of a sentence.

If a parent or teacher finds that a student is misreading too many words in a passage, it is important to evaluate whether or not the reading level of the material is appropriate to his actual reading level. A student should be able to read seventy to seventy-five percent of the words in a passage correctly in order for it to be at his instructional level. If the error level is greater, it must be considered that the material is at his frustration level, in which case it should be changed to a more appropriate instructional level. Once the correct level of material is established, if the student begins to appear annoyed by the request for the rereading of misperceived words, the parent or teacher should switch to recording the misread words. Then, when the student reaches the end of the paragraph or page, an explanation of the inaccuracies can be made. It is helpful to write the two similar words next to each other and ask the student to find the difference in the spelling of each word. The instructor should read each word to the student, and then have the student practice spelling and then saying each word several times, first working with one word and then the other until he appears to have a secure sense of the differences. It is a good idea to put these words on a flashcard for the child, setting them up so that they are side by side, one way on one side of the card, and in the reverse order on the other side of the card. For example, *cow how*, would be on one side and, *how cow*, on the other. In this way, the student will find it necessary to focus on the differences of each word, and will not be able to rely on memorizing the order in which they were set up on a flashcard. As a result, he will establish an internalization of the differences.

If an older student has a visual perception problem that has not been remediated properly or fully, the problem can interfere tremendously with the accuracy of his reading comprehension, and therefore, have a dramatic effect on his ability to handle daily assignments with ease. The student tends to misinterpret written directions. He transposes numbers when copying mathematics problems to his papers. He has a difficult time copying material from his text to his paper accurately, and makes what appear to be careless mistakes. Testing situations are often extremely frustrating for a student with visual perception problems. He misreads directions, words in the reading passage, or the questions that follow a passage, making it very difficult for him to demonstrate his knowledge on a test. For example, Johnny might read "Name five states that begin with the letter M." as "Name four lakes that begin with the letter M." If he reads several words in the passage preceding the test questions incorrectly, his comprehension may be affected so greatly that it will be impossible for him to answer the questions accurately, even if he reads the questions that follow correctly. Visual perception weaknesses can have a devastating effect on a student's work in history, science, English and mathematics.

It is important to note that students who are beyond the elementary level, and even adults, with visual perception problems can be remediated. It generally takes longer, but with consistent work they can greatly improve or eliminate their learning skill deficiency to the point where it no longer severely affects their accuracy. Making these students aware of the fact that they frequently read words inaccurately, or that they confuse similar words, is important. However, it is essential to remember that just pointing this out or asking students to look carefully at a word before they read it, will not cure the problem. Remediation takes time, patience and consistent work. These are essential elements for helping children erase a visual perception problem.

There are materials available for teachers to develop visual perception with their students. However, many of these materials use pictures and symbols. While they are appropriate for students who are not reading, once children begin to read, the materials used to correct visual perception problems must be materials that use words. Children may be able to perceive accurately that a picture of one chair in a row of chairs is facing a different direction from the others in that same row. However, this does not mean that they can perceive the difference between two words such as *have* and *hive*. While picture work is fine as a readiness skill to help children to begin to note details and develop the concept of "like" and "unlike" pictured objects, this skill is often not transferred to the printed word, especially with severely learning disabled children.

Materials that work best are materials that allow the student to note differences in words that are similar such as word and sentence tracking materials, especially those that focus on the most frequently misperceived words. *Visual Discrimination: Noting Differences in Frequently Misperceived Words (Achieve Publications)* and *Thought Tracking (Ann Arbor Publishers)* are two workbooks that provide work in these areas. For example, a row of words may be presented such as *stop stop spot stop*. The student must circle the word that is different. With an older student, more advanced words are presented such as *continent constant continent continent*. Next, the exercises progress into working with sentences, making sure that the most frequently misperceived words are included in these sentences. For example, the sentence may be as follows:

I will find a book for her.

Beneath it would be:

I've I'd I win will while
fine fill find an and a
book look took
from for four he her him.

You can see that many of the words beneath the sentence are similar, but not the same as the words in the sentence above. If this material is used for developmental classroom instruction, the child should read the sentence silently, and then circle the exact words that are in the sentence among the words below. If the material is used remedially, it is best to have the student orally read the sentence and the words as he circles them below so that the instructor can assist the student in correcting errors as they occur. If the student makes a mistake and circles a similar but incorrect word, the instructor should take time to have the child focus on each word pointing out the differences in the words and asking the child to read each one, two or three times. This type of exercise helps a student with a visual perception problem to focus on the details of words that are similar and different, to set his mind on the left-right directionality of word reading, and to strive for greater accuracy while reading.

Remediation must take place on a consistent continuous basis. The material that is used for remediation must be material that is developmental in fashion. Failure in remediation is often due to the lack of consistent reinforcement of the remedial process. Students with serious visual perception problems must have at least fifteen minutes of concentrated remediation, preferably on a five-day a week basis, but no less than three days a week. In addition, throughout the day as students read other materials, if perceptual errors of similar words occur, differences should be pointed out to the children in a kind, patient manner.

It is important to understand that visual perception problems do not correct themselves. Too often parents hope that their children will outgrow their deficiency or learn to compensate for the problem. Neither happens. Instead, what does happen is that the students' deficiencies affect an increasingly greater amount of material as they progress in school. Consequently, their skill deficiencies interfere at an even greater level with their performance in all subject areas. Can students learn to compensate for their disabilities? In most cases, I have not found that to be the situation, especially for learning disabled students. Instead, what I have discovered is that as students become more and more self-conscious about their disability, they try to hide the seriousness of it from their teachers, classmates, and even their parents. As they advance in school to middle school or junior high, high school and, especially college level, they shy away from any situation that requires them to read orally. They even pretend that they have silently read a passage when they haven't read it thoroughly at all, even if it means faking knowledge of the passage. They often do this when they think someone is watching them read. This, of course, contributes to their low self-esteem, frustration level and lack of comprehension of material.

Not all students with visual perception problems are learning disabled. In more than thirty years of experience teaching students with reading problems, I have worked with many students whose visual memory, auditory perception and auditory memory were well developed, while their visual perception skills were extremely weak. In every instance, remediation that focused on visual perception and basic skill development enabled the students to make great strides toward their academic potential.

I remember working with a tall, stately gentleman who worked for a very prominent company as a chemical engineer. He had been with the company for many years and had his doctoral degree in chemical engineering. He came to me at the urging of his spouse, who was sensitive to his problem and hoped that he could receive help at my learning center. During our first session the gentleman told me that he had been frustrated for years by the fact that he was a very slow reader, and that on the job he often had piles of material that he needed to read for his work but never seemed to get through.

I gave this gentleman a complete battery of diagnostic tests. I found that his IQ was extremely high, and that, while his word meaning and reading comprehension levels were excellent, he read very slowly with many minor perceptual inaccuracies. Because he was determined to read for meaning, he frequently restarted initial phrases of sentences when minor inaccuracies were made at the beginning of the sentence and the phrase did not make sense to him. He also paused and reread words further on in the sentence when a word he read did not make sense. There were times, however, when he just skipped over the "little" words that didn't seem to him to affect the meaning of the passage. His visual perception problems were very severe; yet, his auditory perception, visual memory and auditory memory skills were excellent.

It was apparent that this gentleman's visual perception deficiency had been present throughout his school years. He told me that in high school he worked long hours every day on his assignments and was often frustrated by the amount of time it took him to complete his work. He had been determined to perform well in school and go to college, so he spent the time. Because time-wise, it was impossible for him to read entire novels for his English literature requirement in high school, he often relied on Cliffnotes, booklets that summarize the novel, to complete his assignments. But, of course, other students who were perfectly capable of reading the novels used these booklets too, so he didn't feel embarrassed about it. All throughout school he shied away from reading orally. It wasn't until he was in college and his roommates began reading letters they received from home out loud to him or orally read a passage from a textbook, that he began to really understand the impact that his reading problem had on his life. He told me that he did everything in his power to hide it from his college classmates. He would dismiss himself from situations where he knew in advance that he might have to read orally, and made excuses whenever he was unexpectedly asked to read orally. Throughout his college years, he learned to "work his way around" courses that required a lot of reading by signing up for those that he heard did not require much reading. He even changed colleges so that he could go to a college that did not have a literature course requirement. He told me that while he had a great appreciation for good poetry and literature, and often listened to them on tapes, he had never read a novel from beginning to end.

With concentrated work in visual perception development, this gentleman was able to greatly lessen the severity of his problem, expand his speed, and perform at work with much more confidence in his ability to get through piles of technical reading material at a much faster pace. Eventually, he did read his first novel independently from cover to cover. It was *Tales of the South Pacific* by James Michener. I will never forget the pride and excitement that he displayed over reading a complete novel.

It is sad that this gentleman did not have an opportunity to correct his visual perception problem when he was in elementary school. Just think of the hours of homework time he would have saved, the ease with which he would have been able to work in school and on the job, and the embarrassment and frustration that would have been avoided.

CHAPTER 3

VISUAL MEMORY AND BEYOND

Most learning disabled students have serious deficiencies in the area of visual memory. Visual memory involves the ability to store and retrieve previously experienced visual sensations and perceptions when the stimuli that originally evoked them are no longer present. That is, the student must be capable of making a vivid visual image in his mind of the stimulus, such as a word, and once that stimulus is removed, to be able to visualize or recall this image without help. Various researchers have stated that as much as eighty percent of all learning takes place through the eye with visual memory existing as a crucial aspect of learning (Farrald & Schamber 1973).

Children who have not developed their visual memory skills cannot readily reproduce a sequence of visual stimuli. They frequently experience difficulty in remembering the overall visual appearance of words or the letter sequence of words for reading and spelling. They may remember the letters of a word but often cannot remember their order, or they may know the initial letter and configuration of the word without having absorbed the details, that is, the subsequent letters of the word. As a result, these students fail to develop a good sight vocabulary and frequently experience serious writing and spelling difficulties.

Visual memory, in an academic environment, entails work with pictures, symbols, numbers, letters, and especially words. Students must be able to look at a word, form an image of that word in their minds and be able to recall the appearance of the word later. When teachers introduce a new vocabulary word, generally they write it on the chalkboard, have the children spell it, read it and then use it in a sentence. The word is then erased from the chalkboard. Students with good visual memory will recognize that same word later in their readers or other texts and will be able to recall the appearance of the word to spell it. Students with visual memory problems often will not. Once the word is erased from the chalkboard, the word is also erased from their minds, and they will not be able to recall it later. *Later* may be only a few seconds later or days. Without a good development of visual memory, it is extremely difficult for students to learn because visual memory is essential to learning. It is the skill that helps them to store and retrieve information.

Visual imagery is a very important part of the process of visual memory. A child who can create pictures in his mind and has a good imagination will be able to form mind pictures of a story being read to him. This student will, for example, be able to imagine what it was like to live in the colonial days while the teacher talks about the people and their daily lives.

When I was a child, I developed very good visual imagery. Television was not affordable to the general public until the late 1940's. Youngsters read a lot for pleasure, and teachers and parents often read to their children. I remember my third grade teacher reading the book, The Secret Garden, to my class. At the end of every day she would set aside time to read another chapter or two of the book to us. I could hardly wait for the next part of the story to unfold. As she read, I visualized the manor in which the main character, Mary, lived, the robin leading her to the secret garden, Mary's first glimpse of the garden, the garden's transformation and then finally the glorious day when Colin, the once crippled child, took his first steps in the garden. But, if I had not been able to picture in my mind what was happening in the story, the story would not have been comprehensible for me. Children of my generation developed good visual imagery skills. Today, children spend much more time watching television, where images are already formed for them. There is less time left for activities that develop good visual imagery.

Students with visual memory weaknesses frequently have a difficult time recalling the accurate appearance of letters, remembering spelling words, developing a good sight vocabulary, and remembering terms and their definitions. Some beginning readers reverse letters in words or numbers when they write. The difficulty can stem from their weakness in visual perception, which results in the letter, number or word being perceived in reverse or inaccurately. However, there are some children who, even when they do perceive the word accurately, are unable to recall or reproduce it correctly because their visual recall is very weak. Parents and teachers often say to me, "I can be working with Johnny, tell him a word and when it comes up again on the very next line, he does not remember it." Sometimes these parents begin to feel falsely concerned that their child's intelligence may not be normal. "Certainly," they think, "he should be able to remember the word I have just told him!" In most cases, these children have average to above average IQ's, yet are unable to recognize the word when it comes up again, even on the very next line, simply because their visual perception and/or visual memory skills are deficient.

Preschoolers and kindergartners with visual memory deficiencies experience difficulty visually recalling the appearance of symbols, pictures, letters and numbers. As students with visual memory weaknesses advance in school, they sometimes begin to note and internalize the details of pictures, single letters and numbers, but cannot recall the appearance of words, and more advanced visual memory requirements such as series of words, maps or diagrams. Sometimes these students, in trying to compose a small paragraph for their writing assignments, will end up with so many words misspelled that even they have a hard time reading it back to their parent or teacher. Their memory bank of words is drastically low. This can be very frustrating for students as well as their teachers and parents.

Weaknesses in spelling often are carried through into high school and college, even with students who may not be severely learning disabled but may have a learning skill weakness solely in the area of visual memory. I once worked with a young man who was in high honors classes in high school for all subjects, and rightly so. He had an extremely high IQ, was a hard worker, and excelled in every subject area. The only problem he had was his spelling. He was an excellent reader; yet, he often misspelled simple words that he had read correctly thousands of times. How could that be? Well, this young man had not developed the ability to focus on details, the individual letters of words, especially short words that he felt were unimportant words. In addition, his visual recall of these details was extremely weak. I remember when he first came to my learning center he spelled the word *were* phonetically, but rarely correctly. He spelled it as *wir, wer* and *whr*, yet he never had a problem reading the word accurately. Even when reading his own writing, he would read right along as if the word *were* had been spelled correctly. His teachers in high school often ignored his misspelled words, giving him excellent grades on his work. Because he was so bright and his work was otherwise very good, they thought that he shouldn't be penalized for the misspelled words. They were convinced that this, obviously, very intelligent young man was simply not a good speller and never would be one. They thought there was nothing that could be done to help him. This was not correct. Once we began to work with the young man, helping him to learn to focus on the details of words that he most frequently misspelled, showing him spelling patterns, or phonetics behind the spelling of words and training him to develop visual recall for spelling, his spelling improved significantly.

Many people, even highly educated people, are tremendously embarrassed about their poor spelling ability, and yet, they are convinced that they will always remain poor spellers. *There is not one poor speller with average intelligence who cannot become a good speller.* These people just need concentrated training, especially in the area of visual memory, and a strong desire to improve their spelling ability.

Students with visual memory deficiencies, especially learning disabled students, often have very poor sight vocabulary development. Teachers often become frustrated by the fact that they have taught their students the same words over and over again, yet these students still do not remember the words when they come across them in their reading. There always seems to be a few first graders each year who are doing very poorly in reading, and at the end of the year must repeat the grade. Their teachers are often very perplexed about the situation. After all, they have taught these children in the same way they taught so many other children in the class and the other children have learned to read. The teacher knows that the IQ's of these children are at least average, and that the children seem to be trying hard to learn. Their parents have helped at home. So what could the problem be? Since no one knows what has caused the problem, the explanation often is, "Johnny is just immature. He needs to repeat first grade because he is just not ready to learn to read." In the majority of cases, Johnny's attention span is good. He wants to learn to read, behaves well in class, but still is a very poor reader.

Most likely, the answer lies in the fact that Johnny's visual perception and/or visual memory skill development is so weak that he cannot develop a good word bank of sight vocabulary. A child with visual memory weaknesses is often very deficient in the area of sight vocabulary. He simply cannot recall words that he has been taught over and over again. He frequently confuses words that are similar and, therefore, is not able to internalize the words. Sight vocabulary is an essential ingredient for a good reader. At least seventy to seventy-five percent of the material that a child reads should be read automatically, that is based on a solid sight vocabulary. When a child reads he should read fluently, without having to hesitate to sound out each word he comes across. A solid sight vocabulary facilitates good comprehension, allowing the student to focus on reading for meaning. And, of course, a child isn't really reading unless he comprehends what he reads.

Now, it could be that Johnny has a good understanding of phonics but that he reads very slowly, stopping to sound out each word as he reads, but rarely storing in his memory the words that he sounds out. He may be a child who works hard all day, rarely getting his work done because it takes him so long to read a few words. He may read word by word, sounding out each word as he comes to it as a result of his seriously weak sight vocabulary knowledge. If Johnny is a child who does not have a good understanding of phonics, good visual perception and visual memory, he will, most likely, be one of those children whom we label as a "non-reader." He may be able to read two or three words such as *and, the,* and *cat*, but the rest of his reading involves the guessing of words. He, therefore, will make very little sense out of his reading. Often this child's first grade experience is very frustrating for his teacher, parents, and, of course, for himself. Parents often blame the teacher. Educators often blame the inability of the child to learn to read on immaturity. The child is then expected to repeat first grade.

When a child cannot learn to read, yet has average to above average intelligence, it is generally not the fault of the teacher. On the other hand, blaming the problem on "immaturity" just removes the "blame" from the teacher and parents, and places it on the child. Since the cure is not a process that will take place naturally with maturity, the fault should not be placed on the child either. A child with serious learning skill deficiencies simply needs work for the development of specific skills. If a child is repeated, he *must* receive concentrated instruction for the development of his visual perception and visual memory weaknesses consistently throughout the year. Otherwise, he will go through the second year of school grasping little more than the first and, consequently, will continue to experience learning difficulties.

We need to get rid of faultfinding, and instead concentrate on incorporating the development of learning skills, beginning in preschool and kindergarten, into our primary curriculum. In this way, children who are perfectly capable intellectually of learning to read will learn to read well by the end of first grade.

Many severely learning disabled students who were barely able to read more than a few words, were referred to me when they were in fourth grade. Most of these students had already repeated first grade. All of these children had an average to above average IQ, and were children who had worked very hard in school. Most of these children had been given special help at school, yet seemed to be making little or no progress. In each case, after coming to my learning center, these children were able to read at a second half of second grade or first half of third grade level with just one year of remediation. This was accomplished by developing their visual perception and visual memory of words along with a solid basic program in all areas of reading. Auditory perception and auditory memory skill development was also included, if needed. All of this is what made the difference.

Visual memory is specific unto itself. There is one area of the brain that controls the development of visual memory for pictures, another for letters, another for numbers and another for words. For example, a child may have developed a good visual recall of pictures, but not of numbers and words. Diagnosticians must test in each area of visual recall, and educators must remediate each area in which there is a weakness. Some diagnosticians use the IQ test to determine visual memory weaknesses because it has a subtest that involves visual memory of symbols. IQ tests were not designed with the intention of testing visual memory and do not test all aspects of the skill. Very often an older student, one who is in third grade and above, will have developed a fair visual memory for pictures and symbols, but may be very weak in the area of visual recall for numbers and/or words. The visual recall section of the IQ test will not pick this up. Since most work in school involves numbers and words, a child with a visual memory weakness in these areas will experience tremendous difficulties in school. Poor visual memory of words affects the student's work in reading class, and also his work in social studies, science and English. The student cannot readily recall terms for social studies and science. He cannot remember vocabulary and word meanings. He often has difficulty recalling maps, graphs, charts, and tables. Remembering the appearance of words for spelling, especially those that are not spelled phonetically, can present a serious problem for a child with a visual memory deficiency. If a student experiences difficulty with visual memory of numbers, it affects his work with the recall of correct number formation, number fact memorization, and the pattern of number calculation. For example, when multiplying two digits by two digits, he may remember to multiply beginning with the ones and then the tens. However, he may not be able to visually recall the correct placement of the products, or to picture in his mind the format that involves a plus sign and addition after the products are found.

While visual memory skills can and should be taught developmentally to a class of students, this skill is best taught to small groups or on a one-to-one basis in a remedial situation. This allows the remedial instructor the ability to work at the individual instructional level of the students and monitor their instruction as they progress. With consistent concentrated training, visual memory can be developed. I have observed hundreds of children overcome this deficiency.

Unfortunately, very few publishers offer teaching materials for the development of visual memory. There is one company that publishes a workbook that can be used to develop visual memory of pictures, symbols, numbers and letters, called *Symbol Discrimination and Sequencing* (Ann Arbor Publishers). It was originally designed to teach visual memory skills. The teacher asked the students to view a series of symbols, letters, numbers or pictures at the top of the page for five seconds. The students were then directed to cover up the series with a card and to circle the series of symbols, letters, numbers or pictures in the same sequential order among the items below. While the directions in the workbook are different now, the workbook can still be used in this manner. It is a wonderful way to begin the process of visual memory development for a series of isolated items because the length of the series is gradually increased from two items to five items as the students expand their visual recall. This alone, however, is not enough. The real impact of a visual memory weakness is in the area of recall of words.

A number of years ago in my research with learning disabled students with visual memory problems, I noticed that while my students had developed good visual recall of pictures, letters and numbers, they continued to experience difficulties with the visual recall of words. This difficulty encompassed most of their work at school. I realized that if these students were going to be able to develop good visual recall of words, they would need remedial material that used words. I knew that scientists had revealed that in our short-term memory we can hold only six units of information. They had also concluded that the more related the bits of information are to each other, the more likely they are to be retained as a single unit of information (Hittleman 1979). For example, $y\ a\ p\ p\ h$ will be retained as five separate units of information, while the re-arrangement of these letters into meaningful units or syllables, *hap py*, causes them to be retained as two related units making up a meaningful whole.

After several months of carefully observing students with serious visual memory deficiencies, I discovered also that students with poorly developed visual memory were unable to visually analyze a word into its constituent sound units, that is, to break words down into syllables, or to recognize the visual syllabic patterns in words. They were not looking at words in terms of common word parts or syllables. As a result, a word like *spark* would be viewed as *s p a r k* and not grouped into the common word parts of *sp ark*. These students were attempting, instead, to take in multi-syllable words as a whole unit or as single letter units, failing to break words down into meaningful retainable unit lengths. I noticed also that other students with visual memory weaknesses did not look carefully at words. They would look at the first part of a word and then glance at the rest, not taking in the details of words. For instance, words such as *black* or *blank* might be taken in as *bl*, and then *nothing* as the students swept their eyes quickly across the rest of the word, registering only the *bl* in their minds. Other students would focus on the details, the individual letters of the word, but try to take in the words as if each letter were an individual entity. These students would try to take in a word such as, *black* as if it were, *b l a c k* , five separate units. It is impossible for students who have developed a minimal visual memory letter span, for example, of only two units of information, to store and recall longer units of information. In addition, I also observed that some older students with serious reading problems *had* developed a visual memory span for five or six letters, but not for words that were lengthier. For example, a word like *department* might be read orally as *depar* with a slurring sound made by students for the remainder of the word, an indication that the students were focusing only on the first few letters of the word. Or, they might be able to recall the entire first and second syllable of the word only, thus reading *department* as *de part*, but say nothing for the rest of the word.

Children with visual memory deficiencies simply were not viewing and grasping words automatically in chunks or syllables like good readers do. It was obvious to me that their focusing and processing of information was faulty, thereby making it impossible for them to recall many words. Herein, lies the problem of visual recall of words.

Basing my work on this observation, I tried various techniques, and finally hit upon a technique that worked. I began to develop material that forced students to focus on the entire word by attending to the letters in chunks or syllables. I needed to emphasize the importance of viewing words in their entirety, but also to gradually increase the length of the letter span of those words.

It is a lot easier to take in a word like *interesting* as if it were four units, *in   ter   est   ing*, than it is to view it as eleven separate units, *i n t e r e s t i n g* . It is essential for students to realize the importance of being able to group the letters into common word parts or syllables and also to observe the entire word. However, just pointing this out to them is not enough. Students need consistent remedial training to develop and expand their visual recall letter span for words, and it must be done in a developmental manner.

As a result of my remedial visual memory work with students for three years, I realized that I had designed an entire program. The program ranged from a three letter span to a thirteen letter span, and developed the visual recall of students for words from a one-syllable word to a four-syllable word. We began to use the program, called *ACHIEVE: A Visual Memory Program*, at the learning center, keeping statistics on the results with a standardized pre-test and post-test that tested visual memory using nonsense words. By using a test that employed nonsense words, there was no way that my teachers, who were not allowed to see the test, could teach the students the particular words on the test since the visual memory program uses real words and the diagnostic test does not. I discovered that the average student made a sixty-percent plus gain after completing the first four levels of the visual memory program. Why do I say sixty percent plus? I say this because some pre-test scores went below the test gradient. In those cases, the gains were considered greater than the percentage figured and fell in the plus category.

After several years of using the visual memory program, I expanded the program to include five and six syllable words and a letter span that extended to sixteen letters. Ninety percent of the students stayed in the program long enough to completely overcome their visual memory disability. Many ended up with scores far above the average level for visual memory of words. These students expanded their sight vocabulary, and improved their recall of terms and facts for science and history. They greatly increased their recall of the spelling of words and displayed an improvement in their daily work and examinations in all subject areas as a result of improving their visual memory for words. Their progress was tremendously gratifying.

While children with visual memory deficiencies must be offered concentrated remedial instruction for the development of this skill, we must also include step by step developmental instruction for visual memory in all primary curriculums. It must begin in preschool and kindergarten with series of pictures, symbols, letters, and numbers. Most importantly, as students advance in their skills, we must extend the program to include the development of visual recall for words. In this way, we will be offering *all* children the opportunity to develop this essential skill.

CHAPTER 4

AUDITORY PERCEPTION: MEETING THE NEEDS

Auditory perception involves the ability to perceive likenesses and differences in the sound of words. It generally has nothing to do with auditory acuity, that is, the physical ability to hear sounds, but rather the skill of being able to distinguish or note likenesses and differences in similar words. For example, can the student focus on the difference between *clove* and *clothe*, or does he perceive both words to be *clove*?

Some students with auditory perception problems interpret "like" words, words that are identical, as being different. For example, *thread, thread* may be interpreted as *thread, head*. It has been my experience that children with an inability to perceive "like" words accurately often interpret them to be different because the person speaking the two words uses a different inflection in his voice, and these children perceive a different intonation to mean a different word.

Most students with auditory perceptual deficiencies, however, do not experience difficulties with "like" words. More often these students experience difficulties with blends or words that have a similar sound, but are different. For example, the differences between the sounds of *v, th; f, fl; z, sh; m, n; s, sw; s, sh; ch, sh;* and *d, t* often pose difficulties. Words, for example, like *zone* and *shone, favor* and *flavor, saying* and *swaying,* and *way* and *wave* are often confused.

The inability to discriminate between words that are similar, but not the same, makes it very difficult for students with this deficiency to read or spell phonetically. Their comprehension of what they hear spoken and what they read is greatly hindered by their difficulty in deciphering likenesses and, in particular, differences in sounds accurately. Frequently, these students will exhibit the inability to decipher words accurately in their own speech. If you listen carefully, you will note that they often do not pronounce words clearly and accurately. For example, *heavy* may be pronounced as *heby*, and *snow* as *no*.

Since most elementary classroom teachers have been taught to spot children with auditory perception or speech problems, and these children are often referred to a speech therapist at an early age, very few children beyond grade two have auditory perception difficulties. Speech therapists generally work on a one to one basis with their students and do a superb job of helping students to form sounds accurately when they speak. They also focus on noting likenesses and differences of similar words. In addition, they help students to attend to phonetic sounds keenly, thus making it possible for students to utilize well the auditory aspect of learning how to read and spell phonetically.

First and foremost, a student with an auditory perceptual problem must be taught to speak words clearly and distinctly. Parents and teachers of a child with auditory problems need to exaggerate the sounds of similar words, saying each letter or letter combination distinctly. For example, when saying the word *cat*, each letter sound, *c a t,* must be pronounced distinctly, but in the word *sway*, each letter combination, *sw* and *ay*, must be carefully enunciated. It is important to face the student and encourage the student to look at the mouth of the person who is speaking. It is very helpful to point out exactly how sounds should be formed that are difficult for the student to produce. For example, when saying the word *snow* whereby the *sn* sound is difficult for the child to decipher or produce, the instructor should say, "Watch how I open my lips, and how my upper and lower teeth almost touch as I blow out to say *sn*." Describing how the tongue is placed or formed for certain sounds is also helpful for the child. Then the child should be encouraged to imitate the sound using the technique described and demonstrated.

Some students who have difficulties with auditory perception and speech are able to repeat the individual letter or letter combination sounds in a word, but not blend them together. For example, a student may be able to say *sn* and *ow*, but when he tries to blend the two sounds together to say the word *snow*, he says a different word, like *no*. The student may say *sh* and *ut* perfectly, and then put the letter combinations together as *sut*, not a real word. Or, he may say *light* and *ning* and put it together as *lighting*, leaving out the *n*. Blending takes time and practice. But generally if a student watches the mouth of the person saying the word to him and keeps trying to repeat the word accurately, in time, the student will learn to say the word properly. Patience, encouragement, demonstrations and practice are the main ingredients needed to help a student with auditory perception problems.

The instructor who works with a student with auditory perception problems has a good opportunity to teach basic phonetic sounds, which are essential for all students to master in order to be good spellers and readers. All of the basic phonograms (vowel and consonant combinations), vowel digraphs and diphthongs (vowel combinations) should be included in the student's work with sounds. For example, vowel combinations such as *oo* in *moon, ay* in *say, au* in *haul, ew* in *new* and *ue* in *blue* are digraphs, combinations that make a single sound. Diphthongs such as *oi* in *oil, oy* in *boy*, (remember *y* and *w* are sometimes used as a vowel), *ow* in *cow,* and *ou* in *out* are vowel combinations that change from one sound to another. In addition, phonograms such as *op* in *stop, at* in *hat, an* in *can, im* in *him, ash* in *dash,* and *ut* in *nut* should also be emphasized in the program.

Many primary workbooks, especially those that include phonetic skill development, offer teachers many opportunities to teach auditory perception on a developmental basis. In addition, most elementary teachers are aware of the techniques needed to teach this skill and how to spot children with special auditory perception needs. It is important for parents and educators to be aware of how auditory perception problems are exhibited and remediated. Fortunately, however, it appears that this particular deficiency is being addressed very well in most school systems. Most students are remediated by speech therapists with the assistance of classroom teachers before they reach second grade. In addition, children with special speech needs are often referred to outside clinics that specialize in re-mediation. These programs are very effective. What we need now is to address the developmental and re-medial needs of the other learning skill areas, visual perception, visual and auditory memory, with the same intensity that we place on auditory perception.

CHAPTER 5

AUDITORY MEMORY: OVERLOOKED AREAS

Probably the most prevalent but most often overlooked learning skill deficiency is auditory memory. Auditory memory involves being able to take in information that is presented orally to you, process that information, store it in your mind and then recall what you have heard. Basically, it involves the task of attending, listening, processing, storing, and recalling. This, for many students, even those who are not learning disabled, can be an extremely difficult task. A weakness in auditory memory can have serious consequences in the realm of learning for students because students pick up only bits and pieces of what is being said during a classroom lecture. And, auditory memory weaknesses of students can easily go undetected by a teacher. Often children with auditory memory problems appear to be trying very hard to listen. Because their eyes are focused on the teacher and they appear to be attentive, it is easy for the teacher to assume that these children have heard all that is being taught. However, in reality, they often absorb and make sense out of very little of what is being stated by the teacher. As a result, these students recall only a small amount or none of what is being said. They might remember a word here or there, or bits and pieces of the teacher's presentation, but often do not truly understand much of the information presented orally to them. Students with auditory memory deficiencies frequently experience difficulty comprehending orally presented directions. They often think that they have understood directions for completing their assignments, when actually they have understood very little. As a result, assignments are often completed incorrectly.

Students with auditory memory deficiencies will often experience difficulty developing a good understanding of words and remembering terms and information that has been presented orally, for example, in history and science classes. These students will also experience difficulty processing and recalling information that they have read to themselves. When we read we must listen and process information we say to ourselves, even when we read silently. If we do not attend and listen to our silent input of words, we cannot process the information or recall what we have read. Therefore, even silent reading involves a form of listening.

It is important to understand that each aspect of auditory memory is specific unto itself. Students must learn to take in all types of information, that which is presented in isolation as well as in context. While one area of the brain involves the intake of a series of unrelated letters, another involves numbers, another words, and, there are others that involve a contextual series of words, sentences, and whole passages. It must not be assumed that because a student can attend, listen and recall a series of numbers, for example, that he will also be able to recall a series of words.

Isolated units of information are often presented orally in school. Being skilled in recalling a series of items is essential for all students. For example, a teacher may say, "Color only the apples, bananas and pears on your paper." If a student has an auditory problem for series of words, he will not be able to recall the series of *apples*, *bananas* and *pears*. Students need to be tested to determine if they can recall items in a series proficiently for their age. While some students may be able to recall a series of three items, they may not be able to recall a longer series of items. For example, add one more item to the list, *apples, bananas, pears* and *grapes*, and this longer series may be impossible for those same children to recall.

Auditory memory involving contextual information is equally important to the process of learning. Students with auditory memory problems in this area often cannot recall an entire sentence that has been presented orally. Or, they may be able to recall a short sentence of three words in length but not a longer sentence. This weakness poses many problems for students and adversely affects their oral comprehension, and ability to follow oral directions. In addition, while some students can recall a lengthy sentence well, they may not be able to process and recall a short passage that is presented orally. These students may be able to answer a specific question about the information that has been presented to them orally or that they have read, but are not able to grasp the whole paragraph. Often, these students assume that they know what they have heard or read orally, when actually, they have processed and recalled very little of the material. Sometimes parents and educators assume that children have understood an entire passage when they answer a specific question about the passage, yet, that specific information might be all that they have gleaned from the passage. Therefore, students should be encouraged to restate passages, that is, the main idea and supporting details, in order to demonstrate that they have total comprehension. There is a vast amount of information that is lost by students with auditory difficulties. While we want our students to be prepared to answer specific questions from passages they have read, we also need to be certain that they comprehend passages in their entirety.

Throughout my years of testing I have found a higher percentage of students with weaknesses in the auditory memory areas than any other learning skill area, even among those students whom we would not classify as learning disabled. In addition, most children who have attention deficit disorders and/or hyperactivity have serious auditory memory deficiencies. These children are desperately in need of remediation in auditory skill areas

Students with auditory memory weaknesses learn best when new material is presented by means of a visual *and* auditory mode of instruction. Although most of these students have a stronger visual mode of learning than auditory, they do absorb information that is presented by means of their weaker mode. Consequently, when a combined teaching mode is utilized, students take in more information than they do from a single mode of instruction. The ultimate goal, however, should be to provide exercises to strengthen the weak leaning modes of students so that they can use both their visual and auditory modes well to absorb an even greater amount of information.

Sometimes listening skill weaknesses of students are not easy to spot. Adults often assume that children are good listeners when they appear to be paying attention and listening. These children are, indeed, trying their hardest to listen, and because they are not outwardly showing signs of distraction, and look as though they are focused on the adult, it is easy to assume that they are good listeners. In a classroom these children are often very well behaved children who want to hear what their teacher is saying. However, their skill of taking in information, holding it in their minds, imaging and processing what they have read is so weak that very little, or nothing, is being absorbed. If they were to be asked to restate what the teacher has said, even after listening to only one or two sentences, teachers would find that these children are often dumbfounded, embarrassed and unable to restate even the smallest amount of information. These are the children who appear to be ideal students in the classroom but when a test is given or seatwork is to be completed based on the information that was presented orally, they perform very poorly. These children are also sometimes mistaken to be slow learners, when actually they may be very capable intellectually. They are just not able to perform well in the classroom setting because they have serious weaknesses in the auditory memory skill areas.

While there are numerous reasons why children are poor listeners today, one of the major reasons is that they spend too much time in front of the television set. There are some wonderful educational programs for children on television. I commend those parents who encourage their children to watch programs that are educational. However, recently, there have been more and more television programs during the early evening hours that are not teaching good family values or geared toward educating children. I question the amount and quality of time that many children spend watching television and recommend careful selection of programs by parents. In addition, parents and educators need also to be aware of the small amount of information that children with listening problems actually absorb from watching television. Television is not an interactive device and many children have become very poor listeners as a result, even among those who otherwise have very well developed learning skills. Too many children sit in front of the television mesmerized by the sound and fast moving pictures, but not really taking in what they hear or see, or processing the information. No one is asking them to answer questions. No one is checking their comprehension to determine how much they are really processing and comprehending. As a result, we have produced a whole generation of poor listeners, children who are very passive listeners. Television has become, in some cases, their pacifier and not the learning tool that educators would like it to be.

When I was a young child, most families did not have televisions in their homes. Radio was the major source of entertainment in the home, and that was generally turned on only for a few hours during the week. I remember listening to *Sergeant Preston of the Yukon* on Saturday mornings. Stories on the radio were a wonderful source for helping children to become very good listeners. If you were not a good listener, you would have no idea what the story was about. I not only learned to become a good listener, but also developed a wonderful sense of imagery. I could visualize Sergeant Preston trudging through the snow, the wind blowing fiercely as he got on his dog sled. I could picture the dogs and Sergeant Preston covered with snow, and could even envision the breath of Sergeant Preston and the dogs in the cold air. Every sound, the sound of panting, the sound of feet trudging through the snow, every detail was picked up and translated into a message to me that made the story come alive in my mind. Now that was listening!

Imagery is such an important part of listening; yet, very few teaching materials have been designed to help children develop imagery while listening. However, if students cannot form pictures in their minds of what is being said, it is difficult, or even impossible, for them to comprehend what they have heard. Children need to be taught visualization skills so that they can make sense out of information that is presented to them orally.

Years ago, because most children did not have televisions in their homes, and those that did were not in the habit of watching it for hours at a time, there was more time for interaction between children. For example, they would act out spontaneously created plays together that required their playmates to focus on what they heard as the play unfolded. Or, they would create stories that were made up cooperatively by the children as the story unfolded. In order to respond and keep the play or story coherent, children had to be active listeners. As a result, children had wonderful opportunities to develop keen listening skills.

In today's society with both parents often working outside the home, parents frequently feel pressured for time. They need time to handle household chores, take care of the physical needs of their child as well as make sure that they have time for all of the extra-curricular activities in which their child is involved. When a parent asks a child to perform a task and the child appears to ignore the request, parents often become irritated with him and assume he is just not being obedient. If the parent is in a hurry, he or she will sometimes perform the task for the child. Both parent and child end up frustrated and confused. Sometimes, it is not that the child is disobedient or lazy, but rather that his listening skills are not well developed. As a result, it is impossible for him to absorb in his mind the demands of the task, visualize, process and then follow through on the request.

From the time a child is a preschooler, parents should spend time helping their child to develop good listening skills. They must guide and encourage their child to memorize nursery rhymes and songs such as *Mary had a Little Lamb,* and *Row, Row, Row Your Boat*, for memorization helps a child to focus and sharpen his listening skills. The more a child memorizes at a preschool age, the easier it will be for that child to attend, listen and memorize his mathematics, history and science facts once he is in elementary school. Parents need, also, to play listening games with their youngster. There is an old game of "I am going to New

York and in my bag I am going to carry a...." for example, a "toothbrush," in which the child and parent keep adding items, repeating the statement and items, adding a new item each time it is their turn. This is an excellent game to use for auditory memory development. Also, when asking a child to perform a task, parents need to make requests simple at first, having the child repeat what the parent is asking to be certain that he has heard and understood the request. If the request has not been processed accurately, the parent should patiently repeat the request and ask the child to restate it. The worst response that a parent can make when a child is unable to state what has been said is, "You're not listening! You have to listen!" It is very cruel to say this to a child who has an auditory memory problem because he is often trying his hardest to listen, but simply cannot attend, process, and recall what has been stated. Scolding only makes a child more frustrated. The more frustrated a child becomes, the less he can focus on the orally presented information. A child needs to be informed that he has a problem with listening, but in a kind and loving way. Making a child aware of his weakness helps him to want to focus on improving this skill, but since listening is more than just paying attention, making a child aware of his problem will not solve it. A child must be taught *how* to become a good listener. It takes patience and work.

Auditory memory skills need to be included in our basic curriculum, and taught developmentally to every student. It should not be assumed that having a child listen to a tape of a story while he looks at the words in the story is teaching listening. While this type of exercise may help a child to learn new words in the story and understand the story better, children with serious listening problems do not *learn* to listen well by just practicing listening. They need to be taught with exercises that begin at their present listening skill level and developmentally increase in length and difficulty. If a student needs help remedially, one to one or small group instruction should be offered. A good program would include the teaching of specific units of information presented in isolation and in context. When working with isolated units of information, a series of numbers, letters or words should be presented orally to the student beginning at the child's instructional level. The student should be asked to restate the series. If the student is unable to restate the series, it should be repeated until the child can recall the series accurately. Once the student has mastered one level, the length of the series should be increased until the child has developed the series level appropriate for his age or grade. The teaching material *Auditory Sequential Memory Instructional Workbook* (Achieve Publications) works very well for the teaching of this skill, and is developmental in its presentation. While work on the development of isolated units of information is being offered to the child, work with information presented in context should also commence.

Three types of exercises need to be a part of the remedial process for information presented in context. The first type helps the child to develop the skill of listening to sentences that gradually increase in length. The second type is listening to passages and answering specific questions with developmentally presented material. *The Multiple Skills Series* booklets (Barnell Loft, Ltd.) are excellent teaching tools to use for the development of this skill. Even though the material is designed for the child to read silently, in order to use this material for the purpose of auditory memory development, it must be presented orally by the teacher, both passages and questions, without allowing the child to see the material. The third type of exercise that needs to be a part of the auditory memory learning process involves teaching the child to develop the skill of listening to passages and to grasp the *whole* idea of the passage. Educators should work with materials like, *Listen My Children and You Shall Hear*, (Pro-Ed) that developmentally increases a child's ability to attend, process, form images and recall increasingly lengthier passages that are presented orally by the instructor. The instructor reads a passage to the student, and then the student is asked to recall what he has heard. No questions are asked and no clues are given. The student must restate the entire passage stating the main idea and supporting details of the passage. If he cannot restate the entire passage, the passage is reread to him so that he can try once more.

Finally, it is important to focus on the fact that many adults also have poor auditory memory skills. Programs should be offered in the workplace to expand the listening skills of the worker. Often mistakes are made on the job by adults who think they have heard and understood correctly the boss's request, when actually they have heard very little. When a supervisor reprimands his employee for an inaccurately performed job, employees often relate this to others by saying, "Well, I did what he told me to do!" They did do what they thought they heard, but what they heard and what was said, were entirely different. If we could measure the financial loss to a company due to the poor auditory memory skills of adults in the work field, I am sure that employers would be astonished.

There is a tremendous need to better equip parents and educators with tools to help children develop good auditory memory. We must start at a very young age to build this skill so that by the time children are in middle school, high school, and then later in the work force, they are excellent listeners. We must begin by teaching parents and professionals how to spot poor listeners at an early age, and to provide them with the know-how and types of activities that they can use to develop this skill with their children. Most importantly, on a developmental basis, we must incorporate auditory memory skill work in *every* elementary curriculum. We must strive to develop good auditory memory skills in those children who may be deficient in this area as well as to expand the listening skills of those children who may be good listeners but could learn to be better listeners. Finally, we must encourage adults to sharpen their own listening skills by offering them instruction for the development of this very important skill.

CHAPTER 6

EYE-HAND COORDINATION: WHAT IT REALLY ENTAILS

Eye-hand coordination in an academic setting involves so much more than the coordination needed to bounce, catch, or hit a ball with a bat, or to walk on a balance beam throwing bean bags onto an X on the floor. Yet, for years teachers were led to believe that if the physical education teacher could help a student gain eye-hand control by developing such skills, the student's ability to handle a pen or pencil for the physical task of writing would be improved. Educators know now that this is not true. While physical education teachers *did* develop the eye-hand coordination of their students, this was only for gross skills. Students were better coordinated for physical tasks involving sports. Little or no transfer, however, was made to the classroom task of handwriting because the task of handwriting involves finger dexterity and fine eye-hand coordination.

Eye-hand coordination for handwriting requires a student, first, to have good visual perception skills. If a student perceives what he sees inaccurately, he is not going to reproduce it in the correct sequential order. A child with a visual perception problem may, for example, perceive *was* as *saw*, not because he visually sees the word backwards but because he has not internalized the left-right sequential order of reading words. His eye movement may be reversed or erratic. Thus, *was* is viewed as *saw*. In addition, a child with a visual perception weakness often does not note details of words. He may read a word like *their* as *the*, or *sing* as *string*, deleting or adding letters. He may also misread consonants and vowels in words such as *thin* as *chin* or *butter* as *bitter*. Consequently, when he tries to reproduce the word, it is written incorrectly.

The first step to good eye-hand coordination is good visual perception. Once students view words accurately, they must be able to store the letters of these words in their memory long enough to be able to recall the sequential order of the letters of words in order to reproduce them correctly when copying. Thus, short-term visual memory is essential to good eye-hand coordination. Many students with eye-hand coordination problems copy words by looking at one letter at a time and reproducing that letter, instead of looking at a series of letters and holding them in their minds long enough to produce the letters in sequential order. As a result, the task of handwriting becomes painstakingly slow and overwhelming for them. Some students, simply, have never thought about looking at more than one letter at a time when copying a word. These students need to be taught, through practice and sequential development, how to visually take in first, two or three letters of a word at one time when copying, and then gradually to increase their visual memory letter span to take in the entire word before reproducing it. Eventually, the goal should be to help students look carefully at a series of words, and hold the images of those words in their minds long enough to reproduce them without looking back at the material. Mastery of this skill helps considerably to increase handwriting speed.

Some students experience difficulty with the physical task of writing because they simply have not learned to form letters correctly. Students should follow the direction arrows that are provided as guidelines for forming letters very carefully. These stroke directions help students to develop flow and ease with letter formation. In addition, the correct formation pattern helps students to ease into cursive writing from manuscript writing because the pencil ends up at the end of the formation of a letter in the correct spot to connect to the next letter in cursive. Handwriting alphabet guidelines with arrows to show pencil movement directions for proper letter formation are very useful. Parents should obtain a copy of these guidelines so that they also know the patterns, and can use them when working with their children at home on handwriting. Stress should be placed on checking and correcting letter formation, especially when children first begin to learn to write. It is much easier to correct students when they are beginning to learn to write than to try to correct them later when they, for years, have internalized inaccurate patterns of letter formation.

In addition, stress should be placed on the importance of positioning the paper correctly when writing. For the right-handed student the paper should be placed at an angle in line with the student's arm and hand. The arm and hand should be in a straight line using the paper as a guide. Incorrect positioning of the paper makes it harder for a student to keep his arm and hand in a straight line, thus making it more difficult to establish speed and control of writing. Parents should also be informed of the correct positioning of the paper so that they can reinforce the correct procedure at home.

The improper gripping of handwriting instruments compounds many eye-hand coordination problems. Years ago, professionals were very particular about the way students positioned their fingers on pencils and pens. For a number of years, however, educators have become so anxious for their students to just get words down on paper that their concern for correct finger positioning has diminished. As a result, we now have whole generations of young adults who hold their pencils in a number of awkward fashions. Some wrap their fingers sideways completely around the pencil. Many put their third and fourth finger on the pencil. Any numbers of tortuous grips are used. You will see plenty of evidence of this if you go to a shopping mall and observe the young clerks as they struggle to write down a few words on notes or receipts. This improper positioning of the fingers increases the time it takes to jot down a note. However, if you ask these people why they hold the pencil like they do, they will frequently reply, "I don't know why I hold it like that. I have always held it like that. I can't write any other way!" The amount of effort that students put into the physical task of handwriting could be greatly lessened if everyone who works with students would insist that they hold the pencil correctly. *There are very good reasons why we should hold the pencil with our thumb and first finger on the pencil and our second finger underneath, used as a rest.*

In order to make smooth and easy motions, to be able to wiggle our fingers and, at the same time, glide our hand along the paper, this type of pencil grip is essential. Other finger grips do not allow for an easy flow of the writing instrument. Therefore, students with incorrect finger grips often write painstakingly slowly and with cramped muscles. As a result when these students are asked to write an essay, they often turn in an essay that is extremely short. They are the students, who when they are questioned about the shortness of their work, respond with, "I couldn't think of anything else to say." In truth, they simply cannot handle the physical task of handwriting easily so that making the essay short becomes a necessity for them.

When students have eye-hand coordination problems, it is sometimes recommended that they type rather than handwrite their work because, supposedly, it will be easier for them. Students should learn to type. We are in the computer age and typing skills are very valuable. Learning to use a computer is very important. However, encouraging students to compensate for their eye-hand coordination weakness by typing is not the solution to the problem. Learning to type is not easy, especially for elementary school children. It takes a lot of finger dexterity and practice. As a result, it is often very frustrating for elementary students to type their writing assignments, and in the end, many students give up and their parents do it for them. Even more significant is the fact that by encouraging children to type, we are giving students a crutch instead of teaching them to overcome their problem. If we were to break our leg and then were encouraged to use crutches forever, we would find it tremendously difficult later to walk on our own should we so desire. Yet, think of the limitations that we would be facing throughout our entire life, if we were to continue to use crutches! The same is true when we ask children to type instead of focusing on the development of handwriting skills. It is not feasible for students to carry a computer and printer around in their pocket all day for every writing task they face during the day. And, it is not necessarily easier or less time consuming for students. Eventually, for tests, workbook exercises, and chalkboard work, students must use their hands to physically write. Writing is a daily life skill. While some positions require a lot of computer work, others do not. However, even on jobs that involve long hours on the computer, workers still find that they need to physically write as well as type. Notes are often taken during telephone calls or from the computer screen information. While professionals may use overhead materials and other visuals for presentations, at times, they need to write on a chalkboard, especially when they are demonstrating an answer to a question. The physical task of writing is a part of everyone's job. We cannot commit all writing tasks to a typewriter or computer. Therefore, we must make every effort not to provide compensations for students with eye-hand coordination problems but, instead, to encourage students to face their disability and work toward the mastery of handwriting. In so doing, we will be reducing and, eventually eliminating the problem this weakness poses for them in school as well as later on the job.

Special mention must be made of left-handed students. Most left-handed students do have a more difficult time learning to write. It often takes left-handed children longer to learn the task of writing, and they may be more reluctant to work at it. However, some of our best handwriters are left-handed. Left-handedness should not be an excuse for not working on good handwriting skills. Left-handed children need more practice. A reward system for quality practice time can be very effective in encouraging left-handed children, or all children, to practice good letter formation, sentence writing, copying, and speed. Most handwriting teacher guidebooks suggest that left-handed students grip the pencil the same way as right-handed students, and that the paper should be placed at an angle in line with the left arm and hand. While the pencil grip should be the same as for right-handed children, the positioning of the paper and wrist is debatable for left-handed children. Some left-handed children find it difficult to see their work while they are writing unless their wrist is bent and their paper is placed in the same direction that paper is placed for a right-handed person. Others are able to manage with the paper placed in line with their left arm. My observations have led me to believe that the positioning of the paper and wrist for left-handed students is best left up to the individual student's comfort.

While students are generally taught to write in cursive by the time they are in third grade, some children never make a permanent switch from printing to cursive writing. These children often insist it is faster and easier for them to print than to write in cursive. Yet, cursive writing, once mastered, is less time consuming and requires less physical effort than printing. When we print we must lift the pencil between each letter. When we write in cursive, the letters in the word, except for a few capitals, are connected. Cursive writing, therefore, requires less pencil lifting, creating an easy flow and greater speed. In addition, sometimes when students print, they leave very little space between words making it difficult to see where one word ends and another word begins. In cursive writing this problem is eliminated by the fact that the letters of the word are connected and the spaces are only between words, making sentences written in cursive more legible. All students, but especially those who have eye-hand coordination problems, should be encouraged to master the skill of cursive writing and to make a permanent switch from printing to cursive.

Eye-hand coordination deficiencies are remedial. Practice must be consistently undertaken with materials that allow the student to trace, copy, and write by hand, words, then phrases, sentences and finally paragraphs. Correct pencil gripping and letter formation must be checked. The handwriting technique, introduced years ago by A. N. Palmer, that involves students practicing cursive writing by making rows and rows of the same letter connected to one another, is an excellent method for developing speed and fluency of handwriting. For example, the student makes rows and rows of a cursive *f*, connecting each *f* to the next one. Most importantly, special time for handwriting work should be provided daily, especially for primary level students, with an emphasis placed on helping students to take pride in their writing.

Lastly, eye-hand coordination problems should be corrected at the elementary level. The earlier the task is undertaken, the less frustration students have to face, the less likely they are to experience difficulty later with academic work. With practice, and a combined effort to improve visual perception, visual memory, letter formation, finger grips on writing instruments, and handwriting skills, students *can* develop good eye-hand coordination and master the art of handwriting.

CHAPTER 7

IMPROVING WRITTEN EXPRESSION

A prerequisite to written expression is good verbal expression. Does the child have a comprehensive command of vocabulary? Can the child speak in complete sentences, or does he answer questions with one or two words instead of with complete thoughts? Can the child tell a simple story combining two or three sentences in a meaningful sequence? Lastly, can the child compose and tell a more advanced story or talk about an experience in a meaningful fashion? All of these skills are readiness skills that are essential prerequisites to written expression. These skills should be developed at a pre-school and kindergarten level. Once they are developed, the teaching of written expression can commence.

There are many students, with learning disabilities and without learning disabilities, who have serious weaknesses in written expression. Sometimes, these students can talk a blue streak. Yet, when it comes to writing words down on paper they become greatly inhibited. Some educators believe that if students are constantly corrected for every error, and too many red marks are put on their work, they will inhibit students from freely expressing themselves. As a result, there are teachers who have been encouraged not to be too critical of their students' work, and have been convinced that criticism will keep their students from developing the self-confidence they need to write freely. Consequently, we have students handing in papers with multiple spelling, punctuation, and grammatical errors that are never thoroughly corrected, which in turn, fosters students to think that mediocrity is all that is expected.

There is no evidence that ignoring mechanical errors has increased the number of good writers or made students feel less inhibited about writing. James Michener, the famous historical novelist, set a good example of how correction does not inhibit expression. In an interview for a newspaper article, James Michener spoke about his extensive research and how he strived to produce a book that was as close to perfection as possible. He said that as he wrote, he was as conscious about the syntactical and mechanical correctness of his material as he was about the historical correctness of his work. Michener made a point of stating that after he had carefully edited his material, he then hired one professional to edit his book for syntactical errors and another for mechanical errors. Certainly his perfectionism did not stunt his creativity and prolific verbal expression.

What do students need to become good writers? They need textbooks that are designed with developmentally presented exercises offering detailed step by step instruction for written expression development. They need to be taught how to apply good writing techniques to all core subjects. Educators need to be encouraged to set high standards and to be thoroughly prepared for the task of teaching this skill. Since a course in the teaching of written expression is not a required college course for all elementary and middle school teachers, there are some teachers who do not feel confident about teaching written expression. The teaching of written expression should be a required course. College courses should include a step by step developmental approach to writing that includes many teaching techniques as well as many styles of writing.

With writing instruction it sometimes is necessary, in the beginning, to guide students every step of the way. Children, who do not seem to be able to get words down on paper, need to have someone guide them through the exercise until they begin to develop a feeling for written expression. Generally, we begin by teaching simple sentence writing and punctuation. In order for students to write simple sentences, however, they must first understand the makeup of a simple sentence. Even in first grade, students can learn to recognize the difference between a phrase and a sentence. Once that concept is mastered, the writing of sentences should be practiced until students begin to understand that every sentence begins with a capital and ends with a punctuation mark, and they automatically begin to apply this skill to their writing. Children, at a young age, can understand and master these basic writing skills.

Once simple sentence writing is understood, first graders, or beginning writers, should learn to compose a short story of a few sentences in length. Teachers often use an excellent technique called an *experience chart* for initial story writing. For example, after students have been on a field trip, the teacher encourages the students to discuss their trip. The teacher then writes on the chalkboard, or whiteboard, each idea that is expressed in a few simple sentences. The students then copy the sentences from the board to their papers. This is a wonderful way to instill a sense of how we express ourselves in writing. If emphasis is placed on the fact that writing is just talking and then writing down what you have said, students will begin to understand that if they can express their thoughts verbally, they can write.

Once first graders have developed a sense of how writing works by means of experience charts, generally, the next step is to encourage students to write a few sentences of their own on a topic. For example, students may decide that they would like to write about a trip to the zoo. However, just giving beginning writers a topic and then asking them to write, does not necessarily produce results. Teachers often begin by working with their students, discussing what could be written about the topic. A simple outline of these ideas is then written on the chalkboard. This helps to give the students ideas and words that they can use in their writing. It makes them feel more secure about working independently.

If a particular student seems to have a problem starting his writing exercise, questions should be asked that would lead to a response from the student that can be used in his writing. In some cases, the instructor may have to compose and dictate the first part of a sentence, then ask the student to write it down and then complete the sentence by himself. If additional guidance is needed, it should be given. If this is done with the idea in mind that the instructor will, each time he works with the student, encourage the student to participate more and more while the instructor contributes less and less, the student will begin to write on his own.

Once students demonstrate proficiency in writing a short page report or story of a few sentences, longer stories, essays and reports should be required. Many approaches can be used to obtain good results. Models of good essays can be read to the students and discussed. How did the writer of this story express excitement? Did he stick to his topic? How did the writer develop the characters in the story? How did the author conclude the story? A great deal can be learned by examining a good essay, even a very short essay of two or three paragraphs. It is an excellent way to teach children how to write well and to allow them to begin to have a better understanding of good writing.

In addition, we need to stress the importance of having students include words related to the five senses of sight, sound, touch, taste and smell in their sentences. For instance, by using the sense of sound, "The bacon is frying in the skillet." becomes, " The bacon is *sizzling* in the skillet." A sentence can quickly and easily become a more advanced sentence by adding adjectives, adverbs and descriptive phrases. Then a simple sentence such as, "The boy ran down the street to the store." can become, "The tall, blonde-haired boy with the blue-striped shirt ran swiftly down the brick-paved street to Mr. Jones's candy store." Students should be given lists of adjectives and adverbs to which they can refer when choosing words to describe nouns and verbs. In place of the word *big*, students can select words such as *enormous, gigantic, mammoth,* or *immense.* In addition, a list of more expressive verbs can be very useful. Instead of using the verb, *said,* a verb such as *cried, exclaimed, shouted, answered,* or *bellowed* can be used to help enhance the meaning of the action. With just a simple understanding of the use of descriptive words, students, even first graders, can take a very simple sentence and advance their writing level in minutes!

The importance of adding excitement to stories should be stressed. We need to explain to our students how authors add this element to their writing. Having students practice taking simple sentences and adding excitement to them can create results that are astonishing, in only a very short time. For example, "Marissa was running in the forest. She thought she saw a bear." can become, "Running through the dense, green forest, Marissa suddenly saw a large, dark-brown, hairy animal lunging toward her. Could it be a bear?" By teaching simple techniques, we can quickly help students add excitement to their stories and express their images in words.

Most children have good imaginations. They simply need encouragement and techniques that help them to learn how to use their imagination creatively when writing. For children who do not seem to have good imaginations, we need to present exercises to help them form and embellish their imagery skills. It has been my experience that students who do not have good imaginations can benefit greatly by having their parents and instructors read a short passage to them while they have their eyes closed. While the passage is read, the students should be asked to picture in their minds what is happening. It helps to ask students to shut their eyes and pretend that they are watching the action of the passage on a television screen. Once the passage has been read, the students should be asked to talk about what they "saw" and then write it down. Having students draw a picture and then write about what they have drawn is another strategy that helps them to understand that writing is just drawing pictures with words. These techniques help students to develop a good sense of imagery, and to feel more at ease with written expression.

When students are asked to write a story about a topic, they frequently respond by writing about an experience. The stories often are written with, *first* I did this, *then* I did that, *then* that and that. Students need to be guided to go beyond the stating of one fact after another in a dry fashion, overusing the word *then*. They should be shown how to expand their thoughts and feelings, and draw pictures with words as they write. For example, one student wrote the following:

We went to the zoo. We saw the monkeys. Then we saw the duck pond. Then we feed the ducks. Then we saw a parrot talk. The zoo was so fun.

With guidance the story became:

Last week our class went to the zoo. I liked seeing the monkeys the most. They were jumping from branch to branch making a loud chattering sound. They were so funny. We also saw a big, bright green parrot. The zookeeper tried to get him to talk. The parrot said, "Hello. Hello." At the duck pond we were allowed to feed the ducks. It was fun to watch them stick their orange beaks down into the water to get the food. There were brown ducks and snowy white ducks and even some that had shiny blue feathers on their heads. They were pretty. Going to the zoo was fun.

Most importantly, we must go beyond writing about simple experiences and story writing, and include at the elementary level exercises that involve various styles of writing. We need to teach children the skills for writing, for example, processes, explanations, reminiscences, detailed descriptions, conversations, character development, and essays on persuasion, comparison and contrast. In addition, these skills should be broken down into various types. For example, children should have the experience of learning how to write various kinds of descriptions such as: a place, like a city; a scene, like a garden; an object, like a flower or building; a person, like Benjamin Franklin; or an action, like a famous battle. Often educational publishers overlook the inclusion of these important areas of writing in their textbooks. They should be a part of every developmental program for written expression.

Students need to be encouraged, inspired, and required to write reports and research papers, for so much can be learned from this type of writing. Report writing should begin no later than second grade, with simple one-page reports written about factual information that students have learned from their reading or from what the teacher has taught them. Primary level students should choose their topic from selected materials that are at their reading level. Students like being able to choose a topic, and once they begin their research often become very excited about what they have discovered. Using science or history related books that have topics presented on two or three pages, students can be taught to read, state what they have read, and then write the information down in their own words for a short report. Illustrations and a report cover add interest. Once completed, these reports should be read orally by each student to their classmates. In this way, students can learn from each other's report.

Once students get the feel for how easy and fun report writing can be, they should be encouraged to research subject areas that they would not necessarily think about researching. For example, many young boys have a keen interest in dinosaurs. When given a choice of topics that includes dinosaurs, most boys will write reports on dinosaurs. This is fine. However, through report writing we need to seize the opportunity to help students to broaden their interests. If a list of suggested topics is given to the students and they are encouraged to choose a topic upon which they know little or nothing, children will begin to expand their research and gain knowledge in areas that are new and exciting. The exploration of information on grizzly bears, or an unusual Australian animal, can be equally as exciting as dinosaurs. Therefore, we must strive to offer this type of enrichment activity whenever possible. An additional benefit to choosing different topics is that students begin to realize that they, in most cases, know more about their topic than the rest of the class. This helps to develop their self-esteem. And, presenting their reports in front of the class gives them an opportunity to begin, at an early age, to feel at ease giving oral presentations.

As students progress in school, research writing should become increasingly more lengthy and sophisticated. Students in fourth grade should be able to research material using several sources, organizing their information on note cards, and setting up their reports with a title page, footnotes and bibliography. Future inventors, explorers and research scientists have evolved from elementary experiences of research writing encouraged by enthusiastic classroom teachers. Report and research writing must be an integral part of our elementary curriculum. Textbooks that guide teachers with step by step techniques for the teaching of report and essay writing must be developed. If we begin at the elementary level to teach good writing techniques in a developmental fashion, this type of writing will become a comfortable, easy and enjoyable procedure for students. Students will then be prepared for the writing necessities of middle or junior high school.

As students advance into middle school or junior high, and high school, a greater amount and more sophisticated writing should be expected. In recent years, in some schools, fewer and fewer writing assignments, and in particular, research-writing assignments, have been required of students at the secondary level. This is partly because of the large amount of time it takes outside of school to read students' papers, and partly because many students complain about writing assignments. Some of the complaining comes from students who have a poor attitude about homework, but others dislike writing assignments because they lack experience and a solid knowledge of basic and advanced writing techniques. As a result, we are now faced with more and more secondary students who are unprepared for college writing. Colleges, in turn, are forced to offer freshman remedial writing courses, something they should *not* have to do.

We need to offer secondary teachers extra free periods during the week specifically for correcting writing exercises. Textbook publishers need to design writing courses for our secondary students that teach basic and advanced skills in a developmental manner. Most importantly, more colleges and universities should require future secondary English teachers to take courses in basic and advanced techniques for the *teaching* of writing. College courses for English majors often center on developing the teacher's personal writing skills. An English teacher may be a good writer, but still not know how to teach students to write. College professors should encourage teachers to set high expectations for their students. They should encourage teachers to mark errors on their students' essays and to take time to make the corrections. For example, if the critique of a sentence is that it is awkward, time should be taken by the teacher to rewrite the sentence correctly so that the student can learn from the correction. We should not simply circle errors and point out problems without helping students to understand how to correct them. Without specific correction, no learning takes place, and students continue to make the same mistake over and over again. We must, therefore, explain and demonstrate how to correct errors. If a teacher finds that several students have made the same error in their writing, specific lessons on solving that particular writing problem should be undertaken. In addition, colleges need to provide advanced courses in writing for all science and history secondary education majors, not just those who are English majors. Stress should be placed, in particular, on advanced research writing and how science and history teachers can use these advanced skills to help their students.

Learning disabled students need the same step by step instruction in written expression that students without learning deficiencies need. With proper guidance and encouragement, learning disabled students are perfectly capable of becoming very good writers.

Lastly, parents must be encouraged to support teachers in their endeavor to set higher writing expectations. Educators should not have to accept second best from their students, for when that is allowed, that is exactly what we get. Expectations should be high, for when they are high, what we can achieve with students is limitless.

CHAPTER 8

ADVANCING THINKING AND STUDY SKILLS

All too often the inclusion of the formal teaching of advanced thinking skills in our elementary school curriculum is overlooked. There is a general assumption that only gifted children can be taught to develop advanced thinking skills. As a result curriculum designers reserve advanced thinking level materials for the programs of gifted students, when actually all children, even learning disabled children, benefit greatly from work in advanced thinking skill development.

Questions that develop advanced reasoning and thinking skills should be incorporated into textbooks for all subject areas. This material should be designed to stimulate children, from the time they enter school, to think and reason by taking knowledge that they have learned, observations that they have made, and putting the pieces of the puzzle together to arrive at new ideas. Higher level thinking does not develop spontaneously with many children. It has to be taught. With exercises that stimulate the mind, we can advance the level of thinking skills of students, learning disabled children included. The fact that learning disabled students are students with average to superior IQ's (intelligent quotients) makes them perfectly capable of developing these advanced skills. With encouragement, patience and perseverance, they can not only overcome their disability, but also advance their thinking skills to a level far greater than average.

Textbooks should guide teachers to ask questions that begin with phrases such as:

Which is................?
What does...........?
Would you...........?
What is the difference between........?
Does................?
Why are...........?
Give some reasons why.........
In what ways........?
How can you tell whether.........?
Name some objects that........
and Why does.............?

Examples of questions that develop more advanced thinking skills are:

What is the difference between a chair and a bed?
How are they the same?
How are a crayon and a pencil alike?
How are they different?
Does a helicopter fly as fast as an airplane?
Which is closer to the tip of your nose, your ears or your eyes?
How is a microscope like a camera?
How can lakes get fuller even though there has been no rain for weeks?

These types of questions stretch the minds of students, and broaden their scope of learning. Children in every grade, at every level, benefit from instruction in thinking skill development. It should be included in curriculums for all children.

Researchers are revealing more and more data from studies on the subject of raising a child's IQ. Research suggests that IQ is not static, and that it can be increased. IQ test scores can increase, sometimes even drastically, as a child with serious learning skill deficiencies develops these skills. If a child has very weak visual perception, visual memory, auditory perception, and/or auditory memory skills, he simply cannot show his true potential on an IQ test. Since IQ tests are based on perception and memory, serious learning skill deficiencies often mask a child's innate potential. In addition, these learning skill deficiencies interfere with the student's ability to grasp and retain material that has been taught in the core subject areas. Therefore, questions based on general knowledge on IQ tests will often be difficult for a severely learning disabled child to answer. Without good thinking skill development, the reasoning skill areas of an IQ test will also be difficult for the child. Therefore, a child who is learning disabled is often hindered from demonstrating his innate potential on an IQ test.

Jamie's mother brought him to my learning center in June of first grade. Jamie had failed first grade and was scheduled to repeat grade one in the fall. His mother gave me a copy of the results of Jamie's diagnostic evaluation that had been completed in April by the school psychologist. The results of the Jamie's IQ test placed him well within the "low average" classification. Jamie's mother admitted that he was unable to handle any of the material in his classroom, but she was very disturbed by Jamie's IQ score. She saw signs of a bright child at home and was confused as to why his IQ score fell into a slow learner category. She also told me that Jamie's physician had diagnosed him as hyperactive and that Ritalin, a medication commonly used for hyperactivity at that time, was helping Jamie to concentrate better in school. I administered a complete battery of tests to Jamie and found that he was functioning overall at a pre-primer level academically. In addition, he fell below the tenth percentile in all of the learning skill areas. His score on an IQ survey *also* placed him in the "low average" classification. A remedial program was designed for Jamie that used an eclectic but developmental approach for reading, mathematics and written expression instruction. Most importantly, during each session concentrated work for the development of Jamie's visual perception, visual memory, auditory perception, auditory memory, and thinking skills was included in his program. Jamie was to receive one-hour sessions of remedial instruction three times per week.

During the first year of remediation, Jamie's progress was excellent. He made, overall, a two and a half-year gain in a year. By the time he was in the first half of second grade, Jamie was handling his classroom work well. The teachers at my learning center expressed their excitement about Jamie's keen interest in learning. He was now retaining, comprehending and displaying higher levels of thinking about the topics that he was studying. It was apparent that Jamie was not a slow learner.

The school system in which Jamie was enrolled had a policy that all students with learning difficulties must be examined by the school psychologist throughout elementary school, generally every two years. When Jamie was in fourth grade, the school psychologist retested him. The psychologist called Jamie's mother with the results of the tests. He told her that he had never seen anything like this before, and that he wanted to let her know that not only were Jamie's academic scores much improved, but that he had scored well within the "average" classification on the IQ test. Jamie's mother proceeded to tell him that along with his remedial assistance in school, Jamie was receiving remediation at a learning center. "Well," he said to her, "whatever you're doing, keep *on* doing it." So she did!

As Jamie progressed, I instructed my teachers to include study and research skills into his program. By the time Jamie was in fifth grade he was reading above grade level. Jamie's grades at school placed him at the top of his class. By this time Jamie's learning skills were very well developed, and he was producing work two grade levels above the norm. We were now working at an enrichment level with him. At the end of sixth grade Jamie was tested once more by the school psychologist. This time Jamie's score on the IQ test placed him at the top of the "high average" range. This was not a surprise for the teachers at the learning center who could see on a one to one basis how truly bright this child was.

After Jamie completed his work at the learning center, his mother continued to keep us informed about her son's progress in school. Jamie received a high school diploma from a private academy and went on to college. The last time I spoke to his mother she told me that Jamie had graduated from college and that he had become a minister. It is my belief that we did not raise Jamie's IQ, but that we uncovered his true innate potential as we helped him to overcome his serious weaknesses in the learning and basic skill areas.

In addition to thinking skill development, work, study and research skills should be included as a part of the elementary curriculum for all students, including children with learning deficiencies. They need to be prepared to know how to study efficiently from their textbooks and notes. Sometimes students think that digesting factual information and recalling details for tests is all that is necessary to demonstrate their mastery of a subject. Their study skills are narrowly set on learning and recalling factual information that has been presented to them either by the teacher or in textbooks. Yet, so much more is needed. Students need to understand that such skills as drawing conclusions, understanding implications, noting inconsistencies, determining analogous relationships, and comparison and contrast are equally important to their studies. They must understand this in order to be prepared for higher level thinking and reasoning in relation to test taking. Students need to enter middle or junior high school prepared for the task of studying efficiently.

There is often a general assumption that study skills have been taught in the elementary grades. However, most textbook publishers have not included work and study skills on a step-by-step developmental basis in their elementary textbooks. As a result many students are not adequately prepared in these skill areas.

Work skill instruction should begin in kindergarten and involve simple instruction on how to work in workbooks and on worksheets efficiently. For example, children should be taught to look carefully at the entire row of pictures before selecting the picture that they need to circle for their answer. This instruction should expand developmentally to include work and study skills so that by the time students reach middle or junior high school, they have a good understanding of the best techniques for working and studying effectively. Beginning in first grade we must teach students to understand, for example, the use of a table of contents, techniques for memorizing vocabulary words for reading and spelling, organization, and time management. Second and third graders should be taught more advanced work skills and how to study for a test from their textbooks.

Throughout grades four through six, skills for outlining, use of indexes, glossaries, various reference materials such as encyclopedias, almanacs, atlases, and dictionaries should be taught and continually reinforced. These are essential skills that should be a part of all core curriculums.

Most importantly, by the time students are in fourth grade, they should be taught how to read and digest information independently from their textbooks, particularly for history and science. Specific study methods, such as the PQRST study method, that teach students how to *Preview, Question, Read* for meaning, *State* and study for the *Test*, should be included in all fourth grade curriculums. This study method is an excellent technique for students to know, particularly when they are studying from their textbooks. It involves teaching students how to preview the chapter by reading and examining, for example, pictures, maps and graphs in the text and formulating questions in their minds that pertain to them. This piques the curiosity of the students about what they are about to read in the chapter and sets them up for reading with a purpose. Once students have read a short passage, they are then asked to state what they have read, preferably orally. If they can state what they have read, they have comprehended the material. Thus stating acts as a check of their comprehension. At this point students take notes using a shorthand outline format. By stating and taking notes, they are reinforcing the information in their minds twice. In this way they have already begun to imbed this information in their minds. The students continue with this process throughout the entire chapter. They are then ready to prepare for the test using good test studying strategies.

Students need to be taught how to organize their notes and develop test studying strategies. The use of various styles of outlining that help students organize information in an orderly fashion are excellent study devices. For example, charts that show comparison and contrast of factual information help them to sort out the information in their minds and, therefore, absorb it quickly and easily. Research has proven that if students learn to use mnemonics, short cuts for memorization, they will learn more rapidly and retain information longer. For example, if students remember the word, *HOMES*, in relation to the initial letter of each of the five Great Lakes, <u>H</u>uron, <u>O</u>ntario, <u>M</u>ichigan, <u>E</u>rie, and <u>S</u>uperior, they will learn the Great Lakes faster. In addition, they will be able to quickly recall and retain the information longer, and for some students, forever. The use of visual picture aids for remembering series of factual information is an excellent technique for speeding up memory and recall. For example, if students are studying about the causes of the Revolutionary War, the symbol of a dollar sign could stand for the idea of taxation without representation. A drawing of a silversmith's bowl could bring to mind British control of what goods the colonists could produce. A picture of a boat on waves could trigger the idea of the difficulty the colonists faced with overseas trade. In most cases, our minds absorb information through picture or symbol association easier and faster than without clues, especially when a series of related facts is to be learned. Yet, not all students in grades four through six are taught this technique in school.

The development of a good understanding of how to write answers to essay questions for tests should also be addressed. Students should receive instruction on how to determine what might be a good essay question for an upcoming test, how to create an outline for studying all of the items that should be included in the answer to a question and then how to organize an essay properly. Students need to be taught how to answer essay questions completely. Such skills as knowing how to restate the essay question, stating the answer clearly and precisely, and sticking to the question but completely answering the question, are essential for students to learn in fourth through sixth grade. For example, when answering the essay question, "State and explain the causes of the Revolutionary War." a student should not write, "They were taxation without representation, colonial manufacturing, settling in lands west of the Appalachian Mountains, and overseas trade." An essay should include an explanation of each cause so that the teacher knows that the student truly understands the subject. The essay should begin as follows:

> There were many causes for the Revolutionary War. One cause was taxation without representation. The colonists were angry because the British Parliament passed laws to gain more control over the colonies. They felt that they should be able to send representatives to Parliament or be able to vote for the British lawmakers. Americans had grown used to more self-governing. Therefore, the colonists did not like the new laws, especially tax laws that were made without the consent of the colonists. Secondly,..........

The student should then go on to state the next cause with an explanation until he has thoroughly answered the question, stating each cause and explaining it. The teaching of this technique should be included in all curriculums.

In addition to teaching various study and research strategies to students, we must teach them how to organize their study time. Homework guidelines should be presented to all parents and students. Simple suggestions, such as providing children with a homework box that contains all of the supplies such as scissors, pencils, pens, rulers, dictionary, glue, tape, index cards, and writing paper can save valuable time for students in getting their homework done more rapidly. Parents should be encouraged to set up a weekly activity and study time schedule with their children, and stick to it. This helps students to understand the importance of budgeting time. Parents need guidelines, for example, as to how much, or how little to help their children with their homework, how to make homework a pleasant situation through the use of praise and encouragement instead of battles, and how to assure that homework that is completed gets back to school. Parents should be taught the ins and outs of positive homework guidance when their children are in the primary grades. In this way, good habits will then be formed at an early age, setting the tone for a lifetime of positive feelings about study time at home. In addition, parents should be encouraged to purchase reference materials for their children to use in the home such as a dictionary, a set of encyclopedias, and a thesaurus, and to encourage children to use them. While a computer is a wonderful tool to use for research, certain topics and information can be retrieved faster and easier from a book, especially for elementary school children.

The importance of incorporating advanced thinking, work, study and research skills into the elementary school programs must be recognized, for these skills are essential for all students to develop at an early age.

CHAPTER 9

LEARNING A FOREIGN LANGUAGE

The only industrialized nation that does not routinely require high school students to study a foreign language is the United States. While fifty-two percent of Europeans are fluent in at least one other language than their own, only nine percent of Americans are fluent in a foreign language. This is due, in part, to a lack of appreciation of the value and need of learning a second language as well as a lack of consideration of the numerous factors that go into making foreign language study successful.

Students in the United States, for example, are often at a disadvantage when it comes to learning a foreign language. When students do not hear and see other languages spoken and written, they often do not realize the value of learning a foreign language and, as a result, are not eager to learn another language. This is particularly true for students who do not live near foreign countries or in parts of their own country where foreign languages can be experienced. As a result these students do not understand the positive impact that learning another language can have on their future careers. Europeans live within easy driving distances of countries where foreign languages are spoken. As a result, European children visiting neighboring countries for vacations are often exposed to foreign languages at an early age and easily recognize the value of learning to understand and speak a foreign language and its value for future careers.

With businesses dealing, however, more and more with companies worldwide, mastering a foreign language has become increasingly more important for students to pursue. Professionals who speak foreign languages are much more marketable and valuable to employers who deal with foreign companies, and companies within the United States where Spanish is spoken. In addition, there is the advantage of learning a foreign language for the pure joy of being able to move about a foreign country easily, and for the added appreciation of its culture. Learning to speak a foreign language expands the mind, and broadens the horizons. As educators and parents, we need to expose our students to foreign languages as much as possible and help them to realize the value of learning other languages. This can be done by traveling to areas or countries where students can hear foreign languages being spoken, watching foreign films with English captions, encouraging parents to speak, if possible, a foreign language to their children at home, reading and translating foreign language story books to children and purchasing foreign language videos designed for children that present the language in an introductory format.

It is not uncommon for educators and parents to assume that learning disabled students will find studying a foreign language tremendously difficult or impossible to learn. Too often we find students, both learning disabled and those who are not learning disabled, struggling and frustrated when faced with the task of learning a foreign language. The question of whether or not learning disabled students are capable of learning a foreign language often is a concern for parents and teachers. There is definite evidence, however, that proves that students who read at a fourth grade level and above *can* learn a formally taught foreign language. There are, however, two major factors that play a tremendous role in making this possible. They are:

1. The types of teaching materials and teaching techniques that an educator uses to teach the foreign language.

2. The inclusion and teaching of specific work and study skills within the language curriculum.

Let's consider first how we teach a foreign language. It is a known fact that students learn best by means of combined visual and auditory modes. Therefore, whenever possible, educators should present the foreign language lessons using visual and auditory modes simultaneously. When new words, phrases or verb tenses are introduced, educators should make sure that students see the words while they hear them spoken. In addition, the introduction of new vocabulary and sentence structure should progress slowly in a developmental fashion, with new lessons that build upon established knowledge and include consistent reinforcement.

The textbook should be well organized and developmentally presented. Each chapter should include various types of exercises. It should include passages that are written in the foreign language with the translation in English presented next to the passage so that students have the opportunity to develop a preliminary understanding of how sentences are composed and translated. Each chapter should also include the teaching of parts of speech and exercises that allow students to use them. The exercises should include sentences that are partially written in the foreign language with a blank for the student to fill in the correct form of a word. Sentences presented in the foreign language for students to translate into English, and sentences presented in English to be translated into the foreign language should also be a part of every chapter. In addition, exercises that consist of mix and match that involve selecting phrases to complete a sentence and exercises that involve the teaching and matching of synonyms and antonyms are excellent for added reinforcement. Besides basic vocabulary and parts of speech, expressions or idioms commonly used in the foreign language should be presented with the translation in English. Finally, there should be short paragraphs for students to translate into English, and short paragraphs for students to translate into the foreign language. All of these exercises should be based on the vocabulary and parts of speech that have been taught in that chapter or the previous chapters. A textbook that presents various types of exercises in each chapter offers students concentrated experiences with solid reinforcement in the use of the foreign language.

Besides being well organized with varied exercises,

a pronunciation key for the foreign language should be presented in every textbook with examples of English words that have the same sound. When new words are introduced within each chapter, the pronunciation should be presented in parentheses followed by the translation. This offers students a way to independently figure out how words should be pronounced. An example of Italian words presented with the pronunciation might be *scuola* (skwao-lah) school, *teatro* (tay-ah-troh) theatre and *colore* (koh-loh-ray) color. Besides a well organized and developmentally presented textbook, every student should have easy access to a dictionary and book of verbs in the language they are studying.

Foreign language exposure should begin at a very early age. Early exposure helps children to become attuned to hearing a different language, thus making it easier for them to learn simple words, phrases and sentences, and establish an eagerness to learn a foreign language. When children are exposed to a foreign language at an early age, they are much less inhibited about formally studying a foreign language later in school than those who are not.

Pre-school children should be exposed to foreign languages in a casual, playful way. This can be accomplished with board games that have words in English and foreign languages, and by having parents or teachers read stories or have students listen to recorded stories that are primarily in English with foreign words interspersed throughout the story. Gradually more and more exposure to foreign languages should be introduced through simple workbooks and worksheets that focus on the repeated use of new words, and by the teaching of simple poems or songs in English and then in the foreign language. Repetition is essential, allowing children time to memorize and recite words, simple phrases and sentences.

In grades kindergarten to grade three, foreign language exposure should involve a controlled developmental program. It should include the introduction of new words, phrases and sentences that build upon the vocabulary that has already been presented. It should involve reading and speaking, using a combined visual and auditory approach to teaching as much as possible. Children in first grade should begin by copying words and phrases followed by sentences and short paragraphs in the foreign language, and then reading them orally. When children write words and sentences, it helps them to internalize the appearance of the words. This approach is a much better way of developing long term memory of foreign words than by means of hearing and speaking the words without seeing and writing them.

Once a student is in fourth grade, a more formal approach to learning a foreign language is needed. As with all learning, in order to learn a foreign language easily, students need to have good visual and auditory perception as well as good visual and auditory memory skills developed. If a student is not able to look carefully at a foreign word, form an image in his mind of that word, and then recall it when it is no longer present, he is going to find learning any language, his own or a foreign language, very difficult. If a student is not a good listener, he will not be able to recall the words and phrases that are presented orally. Therefore, good visual and auditory learning skills are an essential basis for all learning. Once, however, a student has developed his or her learning skills, one of the most important factors involved with a student's ability to learn a foreign language is mastery of basic study skills.

Students who are formally studying a foreign language must be taught effective study techniques. Foreign language study often requires different study techniques from those that are used for studying core subjects. Too often students think that studying a foreign language involves memorizing a vocabulary list and completing assignments when, in actuality, studying a foreign language involves much more. In addition, they often try to memorize the vocabulary in each chapter of their text by simply looking at the words in the textbook and trying to remember them.

All students, learning disabled as well as those who are not, need to be taught how to study a foreign language. Studying for a foreign language requires an entirely different study approach than studying for a core subject such as social studies and science. Yet it is rare to find a foreign language textbook that includes foreign language study skills. All formal foreign language curriculums should include foreign language study skills as a requirement, particularly for first year language students.

Beginning in grade four, all students should be given instructions on how to study a foreign language. This instruction should be included in the first chapter of every foreign language book and taught by the instructor. Textbooks should also be designed to introduce simple words and sentences and then build upon those words, gradually introducing more and more vocabulary. Since every sentence requires a verb, verbs should be introduced at the very beginning of the instruction. Conjugations of the common verbs *to be* and *to have* should be presented in the present tense and used to build simple sentences. It is essential for students to have a good understanding of English grammar and to have a good sense of diagramming sentences in order to be able to compose sentences in a foreign language. This should be taught and reviewed at the beginning of fourth grade with examples given as to how diagramming helps students to construct sentences in a foreign language. If students understand that a sentence generally begins with a subject, is then followed by a verb and how adjectives, adverbs, and prepositional phrases are used, they can understand better how to use these parts of speech to build sentences in a foreign language.

It is important for the instructor to stress the fact that learning a foreign language does not mean that you just memorize words. It is essential to learn how to compose sentences. For this reason, study exercises that involve conjugations of verbs and the building of sentences should be an important part of homework and required studying.

Begin by teaching Spanish in this fashion:

Step 1: Write a simple sentence in English and then in the foreign language.

Example:
I am going.
Yo voy.

Have the students look at the foreign language words, spell them, and then write them. Then have the students say the sentence in English and the foreign language.

Step 2: Build upon the sentence by adding a prepositional phrase.

Explain that you do not always have to say the, "Yo" for "I" when you say, "I am going" in Spanish. Yo (I) is understood.

Example:
I am going to the countryside.
Voy al campo.

Step 3: Add an adverb to the sentence.

Example:
Tomorrow I am going to the countryside.
Mañana voy al campo.

Step 4: Add an adjective to the noun.

Example:
Tomorrow I am going to the beautiful countryside.
Mañana voy al hermoso campo.

Step 5: The teacher should then continue in this
fashion with the other forms of the conjugation of
the verb such as *you are going*, and *he, she*, or *it is
going*, continuing to add new nouns, adjectives
and adverbs to the students' vocabulary while
reusing words already presented.

Example:
You are going to the countryside.
Tú vas al campo.

She is going to the countryside.
Ella va al campo.

Then:
You are going to the city.
Tú vas a la ciudad.

They are going to a big city.
Ellos van a una gran ciudad.

In this way students have the opportunity to repeat
words that they have learned, and at the same time
learn how to compose longer and longer sentences while
learning words from the other parts of speech. It is a
logical sequence and one that helps students to internalize the language through the use of visual and auditory learning and repetition.

Another teaching technique is for the teacher to
begin with partially composed sentences that require
students to fill in the blanks with the correct form of

the verbs that the class is studying. The exercises should then progress to sentences that are partially written in the foreign language with the remainder of the sentence written in English. Students should be asked to rewrite the sentence, writing the entire sentence in the foreign language. Following this type of exercise, the teacher should require students to write entire sentences in the foreign language. In this way, students gradually begin to build their confidence and ability to express themselves in correct sentence form.

Many students believe that studying a foreign language means memorizing vocabulary words for the test the next day. So the night before the test, they memorize those words. A week after the test, they have forgotten most of the words they had studied. Now the class has moved on to the next chapter where they study a few more words the night before the test, only to forget most of them the following week. Studying by trying to memorize words for the next day's test is *not* how to learn a foreign language. Long term memory is not established when words are studied the day before the test and not used again. The best way to establish long term memory of vocabulary and various parts of speech is to review them over and over again, write them, and to use them in simple sentences continually building on the basis of the old vocabulary learned.

There are several excellent techniques that can be used in studying a foreign language that all students, learning disabled or those who are not learning disabled, should be taught. For example, students should be encouraged to write the new words they are learning in a notebook with the translation beside them. It is also advantageous for them to study the words or phrases by writing them several times, saying the word or phrase following the writing, and then saying its meaning. In this way, they are seeing it, hearing it, and speaking it. This combination of learning modalities helps to reinforce and thus increase students' memory of the language. Also, if students are studying new nouns, they should be encouraged to draw simple pictures next to the words in their notebooks.

Example: house *casa*

The student then writes the word
in a sentence.

Example: *Mañana voy a la casa.*

The student translates the sentence
in English.

Example: Tomorrow I go to the house.

At this point the student should be encouraged to study the sentence by reading it orally, then covering up the sentence and writing it from memory.

In all foreign languages there are words that are similar but not the same. It is easy to confuse these words. Therefore, it is essential to study similar words together, comparing vocabulary words that are similar but not the same, writing, reciting the words and reviewing them frequently. It is also a good idea to have each student keep a list of similar words and their meanings in their notebooks for quick review and reference. For example, in Spanish they might list:

fresa (strawberry)
fresco (cool)

nueve (nine)
nuevo (new)

calidad (quality-worth)
cualidad (characteristic of a person)

asistir (attend or to help)
attender (to pay attention)

sensato (sensible)
sensible (sensitive)

Another study technique that is advantageous is for students to choose groups of words that can be associated with one another and study them together, for groups of related words are learned more easily when they are associated in meaningful units. For example, students might want to make a list of words that are associated with a restaurant. In Spanish, this might include words such as restaurant (restaurant), mantel (tablecloth), camerero (waiter), and carta (menu). Students will find that these word units can be memorized and recalled more quickly and easily than a list of words that are not in an associated group.

Vocabulary cards that have a picture next to the

foreign language word, or a picture on the back of the card, are useful teaching materials for foreign language study. These flashcards are very effective teaching tools because they assist students in making a connection in their minds between the word and the image, and are extremely helpful, especially for learning disabled students.

Teaching words that have a relationship to one another by means of words and illustrations within meaningful categories also makes learning a foreign language easier. It is a known fact that the mind will remember pictures associated with words more readily than words by themselves. This type of study technique is extremely helpful, especially when students write the words and then draw their own pictures next to the words. It helps them to focus on the words and associate them with the pictures of the words within the category.

Example in Spanish:

el cuarto de dormir

un cartel

la silla

una lamparita

una cómodo

un scritorio

una cama

Example in French:

un jardin potager

une tomate

une carotte

un haricot vert

une laitue

un poivron vert

un oignon

Lastly, pointing out foreign words that are similar to English words helps to make the learning of vocabulary less of a challenge.

Example in Spanish:

blusa- similar to its meaning, *blouse*

animal- sounds like its meaning, *animal*, with the accent and phonetic pronunciation slightly different but the spelling exactly the same.

famoso- similar to its meaning, *famous*

While organizing vocabulary in notebooks is an important systematic approach for studying a foreign language, students can also organize words in categories within a word processing computer program. They can add to each category as they learn more words and then print them out for study purposes. In addition, students can organize vocabulary words with their meanings on numbered and colored index cards, using a different color for each category and adding to each category as they learn more words. Alternatively, they can use one color index card for the nouns, another color for the verbs, and different colors for the adjectives and adverbs. These organizational study techniques make it easy for students to review the old words while learning the new ones, and to have a handy way of finding the right word for the building of sentences.

While all students vary in their visual versus auditory modality strengths, all students learn best by means of a combined visual *and* auditory approach. In addition, a tactile and kinesthetic approach to learning a foreign language, which involves asking students to write the words, helps tremendously to reinforce learning. An excellent visual, auditory, tactile, and kinesthetic (VAKT) study approach is to have students:

1. Visually examine a word, noting the spelling of the beginning, middle and the end of the word and spell it orally.

2. Write the word from memory.

3. Say the word aloud in the foreign language and then say its meaning in English.

4. Close their eyes and visualize the word.

5. Look at the word again to be sure their visualization of the spelling is correct.

6. Turn the paper over and write the word from memory.

7. Write the word in a sentence.

Note: If a particular word is difficult to learn, the student can trace the word over and over again, saying the letters as he traces them and then saying the word in the foreign language and its meaning in English.

Vocabulary knowledge is entered into short term and long term memory through effective memorization techniques and review. In order to establish long term memory of vocabulary, it is essential to consistently use memorized vocabulary in various types of exercises. These exercises should include oral and written work, and practical usage of the language. It also involves regular review until the recall of words, common phrases and sentences are comfortable and feel natural. It is extremely important for students to work on the easy words first and then to build upon that knowledge, and to concentrate most of their time and effort on the words that they find more difficult to remember. A good rule of thumb is for students to be encouraged to review the material they are studying beginning with 10 minute intervals throughout the study hour, then hourly intervals throughout the next three to four hours, and finally daily intervals, until they feel confident that they have learned the material.

Foreign language workbooks that present the language in a developmental manner with exercises built on what has been taught in the text are an excellent source to use to reinforce each lesson. The workbooks should include filling in the blanks with the correct part of speech, composing and writing sentences in the foreign language, translating from the foreign language into English and English to the foreign language, and orally composing and reciting sentences in the foreign language.

Students should also be encouraged to try to speak the language to one another in small groups talking about various topics that are based on the material taught in the lesson. For example, if the teacher has been teaching the students words that are useful for a visit to a restaurant, students might pretend that one person is the waiter and the others are the customers ordering from the menu. They should be encouraged to make up a conversation whereby they ask to be seated, ask for the menu, ask questions about the foods on the menu, order their meal and ask the waiter for additional foods or utensils. They should plan this by deciding what they want to include in English first, then in the foreign language, and then exactly what they are going to say and who is going to say it. They should then write down their conversation, practice it orally and then recite it in class without reading it. In this way, the learning that takes place is a well planned organized lesson in which everyone in the group truly learns.

In addition, students should be required to practice reading sentences orally in the foreign language as a part of their homework assignment. The teacher might also suggest that they audio or video record themselves speaking the language. In this way, students begin to hear themselves speaking the foreign language at home, in a relaxed environment. This, in turn, helps them to increase their confidence and feel more at ease when they are asked to speak in class.

As students progress in the learning of a foreign language, they should be encouraged to listen to foreign language audio recordings and CD's that include printed material of the recordings, and to watch videos in the foreign language that have the English translation in captions. The audio and video recordings should be those that are designed for beginners so that the language is progressively introduced. As students progress further in their study of the foreign language, videos without captions can be introduced. While initially students may feel that the person speaking the foreign language is speaking too rapidly for them to understand, they will find that if they play the video over and over again, they will comprehend more and more. Surprisingly, as they begin to concentrate on what the person is saying and "tune" their ears to the sound of the language or the person speaking, they will understand more and more, until the speaker does not seem to be speaking rapidly at all.

While studying a foreign language takes time and devotion, with an organized approach that includes good teaching materials and techniques along with the teaching of good study skills, students, including learning disabled students, can achieve the joy, pride, satisfaction and mastery of the learning of a foreign language.

Chapter 10

THE BEST MATHEMATICS APPROACH

A *dyslexic* child is one who experiences learning problems in the language areas only. A *learning disabled* child is one who experiences learning problems in the mathematics and language areas. Mathematical disabilities are often referred to as *dyscalculia* which involves all types of mathematics problems such as difficulty in understanding the meaning of numbers and their spatial relationships, and an inability to apply and process formulas and word problems.

Students with deficiencies in mathematics often have serious weaknesses in the learning skill areas of visual and auditory perception, but in particular with visual and auditory memory. These weaknesses severely hinder their ability to perform well in mathematics. When students copy numbers incorrectly or write numbers in reverse, for example, writing a 3 as an E, it is often an indication that there is a weakness in visual perception and/or visual memory. Difficulties with memorization of facts or the memorization of the basic steps of mathematical processes that have been presented to students visually can also be an indication that there is a weakness in visual memory. In addition, auditory memory plays an important role in the ability of students to attend, listen and recall, for example, a series of numbers or a multiplication fact that has been presented to them orally by the teacher. Learning disabled students who experience difficulties in mathematics must, therefore, receive concentrated work for the development of visual and auditory memory and perception as a foundation for basic mathematics skill remediation.

Along with the concern for the effect of weak learning skills, it is equally important to concentrate on all three major areas of mathematics: basic concepts, computation and application.

BASIC CONCEPTS

Basic concept development involves the ability to comprehend the spatial relationships of numbers. Does the student have a good grasp of the patterns of numbers, the evenness of numbers? How far apart are 2, 4, 6, 8, and 10? Can the student fill in the missing numbers for a pattern of numbers, such as 3, ___, 9, 12 or 22, 33, ___, 55? Once a student begins to acquire a good feeling for patterns of numbers, he will be better equipped to handle, for example, mental mathematic problems that require calculation in his mind without having to use paper and pencil.

The second area of concept development involves having a good understanding of basic fractions such as dividing a whole into parts or understanding how the parts fit together to make the whole. Even preschoolers can begin to understand the concept, for example, of cutting an orange down the middle and how the two halves make a whole. Parents should be encouraged to help their children develop an understanding of basic fraction concepts by having them learn how to follow a simple recipe using a one cup measuring cup and finding fractions of the whole. Children should also be encouraged to develop a sense of fractions using a ruler to find an inch, half inch, quarter of an inch or twenty millimeters, ten millimeters, and then five millimeters.

Lastly, students must have a good concept of mathematical symbols. Learning disabled students often confuse or are uncertain of the meaning of common mathematical symbols. For example, they may confuse the + and − signs, or not know that the ÷ sign means to divide. They may not understand that the symbols × and * mean to multiply, or that the term *take away* is synonymous with *minus*. If instructors use these synonymous symbols or terms interchangeably, they must be certain that their students understand that these symbols and mathematical terms are indicators for the same mathematical operation.

COMPUTATION

The second basic area of mathematics is computation which includes addition, subtraction, multiplication, division, fractions, percents, mental computation and numerical reasoning. Mental computation involves the ability to attend to an orally presented number combination that is to be calculated, form images in one's mind of those numbers, hold those numbers in one's mind and calculate the answer. Exercises to train the mind for this multifaceted process are essential for all students but, in particular, for learning disabled students. Initially, flashcards with the numbers to be calculated can be viewed by the students in combination

with the oral presentation. As students become proficient in mental computation with visual aids, number
problems should be presented orally without visual aids
so that students can learn how to handle mental computation solely with an oral presentation.

Numerical reasoning generally involves basic al-
gebraic equations. This form of computation begins
with simple problems such as $3 + \square = 5$ and advances
to basic algebra. Being able to understand basic mathematical facts and how to balance the numbers to the
left of the equal sign so that they equal the number or
numbers to the right of the equal sign, is essential. It
involves a good understanding of basic number concepts including the spatial relationships of numbers.

APPLICATION

Application, the third basic area of mathematics,
involves money, measurement, time, word problem
solving and a good understanding of the elements necessary for being able to calculate the answer to a word
problem. For example, if a student wants to figure out
how much taller Megan is than Michelle, the student
needs to know that they cannot possibly answer the
question unless they have all of the mathematical facts
that they need, which in this case is the height of both
girls. Or, the student needs to be able to reason that if
each child in the class needs four crayons, he needs to
know how many children there are in the class in order
to figure out how many crayons are needed in total.

Word problem solving should be an integral part
of each computational skill that is taught. Understanding

the practical application of mathematics makes it real, and helps students to understand the necessity of learning mathematical calculations and formulas. All too often, there is an insufficient amount of word problems included in mathematics textbooks. For this reason, a supplemental workbook of word problems should be supplied with every textbook. This workbook should be designed to reinforce the mathematical skills taught in the textbook, including a mixture of word problems that include review of the skill previously taught with the new one. This requires students to switch from one type of calculation to another. For example, if subtraction of two digit numbers by two digit numbers was just taught, word problems involving the subtraction of two digit numbers by two digit numbers should be presented, with the interspersing of addition of two digit by two digit numbers. The more learning disabled students are made to switch their thinking from one type of problem to another, the easier it becomes for them to make those changes. All students, but in particular, learning disabled students, need to be taught to think carefully about word problems, analyze them, and then determine what process is needed in order to solve the word problem. By switching from subtraction to addition, and addition to subtraction, students learn to change their thinking from one mode of calculation to another, thereby recognizing the importance of determining the correct process needed to solve a problem before they can begin to calculate the answer.

All too often learning disabled students experience difficulty in the area of application that involves money. The main reason for this difficulty is that they have not had consistent training and reinforcement in this area. Mathematics workbooks and textbooks often have only a few pages devoted to money, not enough for most students, particularly learning disabled students. When working remedially with students on money, the first step is to make certain that they can identify coins and that they know the value of those coins. It is extremely helpful for children to understand that a quarter is worth 25 cents, two quarters equals 50 cents, and that four quarters equals a dollar. It is important for children to memorize that one hundred pennies, ten dimes and twenty nickels are also equal to a dollar. Children often do not understand how to count money because they do not have a good concept of the amount of money that makes up a dollar. Once the value of coins is taught, flashcards containing the amount of pennies, dimes, quarters, and then nickels that equal one dollar should be made. Children should be encouraged to memorize these money facts. Once students are able to identify coins and have a basic concept of like coins that make up the dollar, they need to be taught how to switch from counting, for example, by 10's with dimes, to 5's with nickels. Gradually, as students progress, the counting of two different coins should be increased to counting three different coins, such as from dimes to nickels to pennies. Frequent review and experience with counting money should be a consistent part of students' work, until the concept is internalized to the point where they no longer need review. At home, children should be encouraged to have a piggy bank, to count their savings frequently and to open a savings account at a bank so that they can watch their statements to see how their money grows. Another good way to give children experience in counting money is for parents to empty their pocket or change purse and ask their children to count the change. If parents offer to give part of the change to their children if they count it accurately, it makes counting the money even more exciting for them. The best way for children to truly gain a good understanding of money is for them to have consistent review, and occasions for them to use money on a regular basis.

The telling of time is often a skill that appears to be difficult for learning disabled students to master. The main reason for this difficulty is that there are generally just a few pages in a mathematics textbook dealing with time. When children are exposed to a new concept and then it is not consistently reviewed and used, it is easy for them to forget what they have been taught. For this reason, educators should frequently include work involving telling time and offer frequent practice by requiring students to tell time on a casual basis throughout the school year. Parents should be encouraged to reinforce this skill at home by asking their children to tell time at home on a frequent basis, thus providing their children with continuous practical experience for the mastery of this skill.

The teaching of telling time must be done in a systematic fashion beginning with an understanding that there are twenty-four hours in the day but that the clock shows only twelve hours. Therefore, the hands of the clock must go around twice during the day to equal the twenty-four hour period. Time should be taught beginning with time on the hour, then half hour, and quarter hour, pointing out that the clock is like a pie that can be cut into four quarters. Once children have mastered the four quarters, that is, fifteen minutes after, thirty minutes after, and then forty-five minutes after the hour, it is important to begin teaching the telling of time by five minute intervals and then minute intervals. At the same time that children are learning to read time on the clock, they should also be asked to demonstrate that they understand the concept being taught by moving the hands on a cardboard clock to given times. For example, students might be asked to set the clock at 2:20, 5:15 and 3:35. This helps to provide practice through hands-on application. Besides mastering the telling of time, students need practice with word problem solving that involves time. If, for example, Jack is at the movie theatre at 2 pm and the movie starts at 2:15 pm, how long will it be before the movie starts? Parents should be encouraged to have analog clocks in their homes and to buy their children analog watches with Arabic numbers on them, instead of commonly used digital clocks and watches. In this way children can observe how the hands move around the analog clocks and watches, thus developing a better feeling and understanding of time periods. A sense of time is essential for children to learn so that the scheduling of enough time for assignments, various sections of tests, and being ready on time can be established.

The final area of mathematics application is related to measurement which includes linear (distance), weight and temperature. The United States, Liberia, and Myanmar (Burma), are the only three countries in the world where the English system of measurement is the primary system of measurement. Every other country in the world uses the metric system of measurement. Within the United States everyday measurement based on the old English system which uses pounds, feet, and miles is commonly taught and used, while metrics is taught as a secondary means of measurement. Consequently, in the business world in the United States, engineers, architects and professionals who work for companies who deal with foreign countries must record their measurements in two systems, the English system and the more accepted world-wide metric system. The United States has not restricted the use of metrics. The problem lies in the fact that manufacturers in the United States have not made a real effort to make the transition to metrics, while other countries have done so successfully and with a relatively smooth transition by simply packaging and labeling goods in metrics. The reluctance to change to metrics in the United States is mind boggling. In the United States the liter and two liter bottle of soda appears to be the only transition that has been made. No one seemed to mind that transition. The change was not difficult for most Americans to accept. It is the kind of conversion that should be done with all packaged products. Unfortunately, further progress in making the change has not been attempted. The major problem that this presents in education is that all students in the United States must learn both the English and metric system. However, since the metric system is not commonly used, it is rarely mastered. For most students in the United States, and especially for learning disabled students, metrics remains a non-mastered skill. For once students are taught metrics, they have little or no common use of the system and, therefore, find it hard to comprehend and internalize. The switch to metrics is long overdue. Now is the time for educators to insist that the metric system of measurement be the primary system of measurement used in the United States, thus allowing educators and students to concentrate solely on the metric system of measurement.

While the metric system is a system that is based on tens and is, therefore, far easier to learn and master than the English system, whether or not an educator is teaching the English or metric system, the secret to aiding a learning disabled student in this area is to expose students to a hands-on approach to the learning of measurement. Students should be required to memorize common units of measurement, presented with examples of how they are used on an everyday basis, given exercises in measuring and asked to solve problems related to measurement. Unfortunately, until the United States makes a complete switch to the metric system, the English *and* metric units of measurement will have to be taught in school.

Parents should be encouraged to work with their children at home with practical everyday uses of measurement. For example, parents might ask their children to measure the width of a wall to determine if the width of a bookcase that is to be placed in the room will fit, to measure the floor of their bedroom to determine the amount of new carpeting that is needed, or to measure the height of a pole that is to be installed in the backyard to hold a birdhouse. Boys and girls should be allowed and encouraged to learn to bake and to learn how to follow the recipes by making exact measurements. Parents should give children a one cup measuring cup instead of pre-measured cups so that their children can find, for example, 1/2 or 3/4 of a cup, and visually understand parts of a whole. A cookbook that gives the metric units of measurement with an

English equivalency chart in the back of the book is also advantageous for children to use. Children should be encouraged to convert the metric recipe to the English measurement and then as they progress in cooking to try the same recipe using the metric measurement. Parents should also encourage their children to participate with them in projects that involve measuring such as scrap booking or woodworking in order to help children gain a good solid practical understanding of the uses of measurement.

In regard to units of weight, parents should be encouraged to have their children use a scale and to talk about the weight of an infant versus a child their age, or versus an adult. When shopping at the grocery store, parents should ask children to read the weights of items that are being purchased. If, for example, children are asked to put a five pound bag of flour in the shopping cart and then a one pound can of coffee, they will begin to get the feel for how heavy five pounds is, compared to something that weights one pound. Asking children to then look for the metric weight equivalent of each item that is written on the package after the English unit, helps them to begin to learn about metric weights and volumes. While most items in the grocery stores in the United States are packaged by the English system of measurement, the metric equivalent generally does follow the English measurement on most items.

Temperature also should be taught, with practical application being a key factor. Parents should be encouraged to have an indoor/outdoor English/metric thermometer in their home and to encourage their children to check the temperature in both systems when deciding if it is cool enough to warrant putting on a light jacket or a heavy coat. Children should be encouraged to watch the weather channel and notice, for example, what the high and low temperatures are in the forecast. Unfortunately, most United States television meteorologists present the forecasted temperatures in the English system only instead of, or along with, the metric system. When teaching students temperature, teachers should encourage children to take turns presenting the weather forecast for the day in both systems.   Until the switch to metrics is made in the United States, this type of dual practice exercise will be needed. In addition, students should be taught, for example, the temperature at which water freezes and boils and asked to memorize these facts in both the English and metrics. While measurement should be taught and applied to practical everyday uses in school, practical application and reinforcement of these skills at home by parents is essential for the mastery of the skill of measurement.

Working with students who experience serious problems with mathematics as well as language related subjects can seem overwhelming for parents and teachers. It can be frustrating for parents and teachers, for instance, when they work with learning disabled students on fact memorization flashcards and find that their children know the answers one day and not the next. Some learning disabled students appear to have no mathematical sense, leading teachers and parents to throw up their hands in dismay and conclude that teaching these children mathematics is an impossible task. However, it has been my experience that with work for the development of basic learning skills along with the correct type of teaching techniques for the development of basic skills, and perseverance, a breakthrough with learning disabled students can be made. For once the basic learning and mathematical skills are developed, these children can learn mathematics just like any other child.

Jeffrey came to me when he was eight years old. He was severely hyperactive and on medication that helped him to sit more quietly at his desk and concentrate. At times, he exhibited rhythmic movement of his hands and shuffling of his feet. However, despite this need for movement, Jeffrey was very cooperative and eager to improve his skills. Jeffrey's mathematics skills were, however, at a beginning first grade level. For one month we worked on establishing his understanding of the basic concept of addition up to ten, using pegs, dominoes, pencils, and beads. At the same time concentrated work for the development of visual and auditory perception and memory were included in his program. Once Jeffrey seemed to understand the concept of addition with objects, we progressed to the memorization of number facts. Jeffrey was given a few flashcards to study at home with his parents. They had the fact on one side of the card without the answer, and the fact with the answer on the other side of the card. Each time Jeffrey returned to class, however, he came back with very few flashcards memorized.

I decided to try using the VAKT technique with Jeffrey whereby he would trace the numbers saying the numbers as he traced them over and over again until he thought he truly knew the fact. He did this over and over again with only two number facts during each session. It seemed, at first, like this particular child was not going to be able to memorize the facts like most learning disabled students did when I tried the VAKT technique, but we persevered. Suddenly, after two months there was a breakthrough and Jeffrey was able to recall the correct answers to the facts from memory! After that, the learning process for all mathematics went much smoother and Jeffrey was able to process mathematical functions with much more ease.

With constant persistent use of the VAKT technique Jeffrey's brain was being patterned to process the format of number facts. It was like "putting the needle in the groove," and once that was accomplished, Jeffrey was able to understand and sort in his mind the processes needed to memorize and understand mathematical number facts.

Of the hundreds of students with learning disabilities with whom I have worked, Jeffrey was the most severely mathematically learning disabled student. Yet, once the break-through was made, Jeffrey was able to overcome his learning disability, moving on to meet all of the basic mathematical requirements. He eventually graduated from high school and went to a two year college majoring in horticulture.

In addition to fact memorization, another serious mathematical weakness that is exhibited by learning disabled students is a lack of understanding of the spatial relationships of numbers, the evenness of numbers or the pattern of numbers. If students have a good feeling for the patterns of numbers such as how far apart are 2, 4, 6, 8, 10 or 3, 13, 23, 33, they will have a good number sense and foundation for mental computation, comprehension of basic mathematical calculations and word problem solving. Therefore, exercises with a simple number chart involving the teaching of patterns of numbers is essential.

Example of chart:

1	2	3	4	5	6	7	8	9	10
11	12	13	14	15	16	17	18	19	20
21	22	23	24	25	26	27	28	29	30
31	32	33	34	35	36	37	38	39	40
41	42	43	44	45	46	47	48	49	50
51	52	53	54	55	56	57	58	59	60
61	62	63	64	65	66	67	68	69	70
71	72	73	74	75	76	77	78	79	80
81	82	83	84	85	86	87	88	89	90
91	92	93	94	95	96	97	98	99	100

Because learning disabled students often do not note patterns of numbers that are obvious to others, patterns need to be pointed out to students. For example, instructors need to point out the fact that all of the numbers in the first column of the table above end with a one, while the next column ends with a two, then a three, etc. until we reach the zero column. Having students read the numbers in a column to see that first there is, for example, a 5, then a 15, 25, 35, 45, 55 etc. up to 95 helps them to understand the concept of tens, and to recognize the pattern and spatial relationships of numbers. Many exercises can be used with the chart such as teaching students how to count by tens, fives, and then twos. Educators can also have students start at a given number and then count forward three, four or five more numbers so that students visually begin to understand the concept of addition, or count backwards three, four or five numbers to get the feeling of subtraction. This chart should be posted where students can see it at all times, until they begin to internalize the patterns of numbers.

An excellent way to help students calculate the answers to addition and subtraction problems, when they are beginning to learn these skills, is to use a picture of a ladder with ten rungs.

Example of Ladder:

Students should be taught that addition involves moving up the ladder and subtraction is moving down the ladder. If they picture themselves climbing up the ladder and down the ladder, learning disabled students begin to get a better feeling for what addition and subtraction are all about. If the number problem is "3 + 4 = ___" , the student should be taught to begin at the third rung, saying 3 and then counting up 4 more steps, saying "4, 5, 6, 7. The answer to 3 + 4 is 7." In subtraction, students should take the highest number and move down the ladder. For example, with 7 − 4 =___ , they should start at the 7th rung and move down 4 rungs saying, "6, 5, 4, 3. The answer to 7 − 4 is 3." Learning disabled students seem to be able to understand and internalize the concept of addition and subtraction better with a ladder than by using the number line that is often used for initially teaching addition and subtraction to students. It may be because they acquire a better sense of numbers getting higher with addition and lower with subtraction on the ladder than with the horizontal back and forth movement on a number line. Consistent and concentrated work with addition and subtraction facts should begin with the ladder. However, it is important to transfer this to fact memorization with flashcards so that students do not need to rely on having to calculate the facts on a long term basis.

If students continue to experience difficulties with memorization of certain mathematical facts, the VAKT technique should be used. The VAKT technique, as mentioned above in the case study of Jeffrey, involves having students trace the number fact as they say it over and over again, until they feel that they truly know it. Students should then turn the paper over and write the fact from memory. This technique uses the Visual, Auditory, Kinesthetic and Tactile (VAKT) approach allowing students to see, hear, get the motion, and feel of the related numbers. It patterns the brain and imbeds in their minds the series of numbers that "go together" to make up that number fact. The VAKT technique can be very effective when used to help students internalize specific facts that are difficult for them to memorize. It is important to note, however, that for all students, and particularly learning disabled students, frequent review of number facts is essential for the development of long term fact memorization.

Another excellent approach to use with students

who experience difficulties with mathematics is to incorporate concentrated work with *number families* into the program. Number families consist of three numbers that go together to make two addition and two subtraction facts. When using this technique, it is helpful to tell students that a number family consists of a *mother, father, sister*, and *brother*. Mother and father are the addition facts, while sister and brother are the subtraction facts. It is helpful also for instructors to point out to students that when we *add*, the largest number of the number family is at the *end* of the fact but when we *subtract,* the largest number comes first and *begins* the fact. Providing "tricks"for remembering mathematical functions and processes is extremely effective in helping all students, learning disabled and those who are not, learn and recall mathematical facts and functions quickly and effectively. "Tricks" are effective aids to long term memory development.

Example of a Number Family:

5, 3, 8

Addition:	Subtraction:
Mother: 5+3=8	Sister: 8–5=3
Father: 3+5=8	Brother: 8–3=5

Using this technique, work on all the basic facts teaching students that if they know that 5, 3, and 8 are the numbers that go together in this family, they can name the addition and subtraction facts for these numbers very easily. Number families can also be used with multiplication and division facts.

Example of a Number Family:

3, 2, 6

Multiplication:	Division:
Mother: 3x2=6	Sister: 6÷2=3
Father: 2x3=6	Brother: 6÷3=2

All students should be given a number chart that consists of number facts presented in rows from one to nine for addition, subtraction, and then later for multiplication and division so that they can see the patterns and spatial relationships of the numbers. These charts should be examined carefully by students with the teacher pointing out the patterns and spatial relationships of the number facts. For example, it should be pointed out that once students learn, for example, that 4+6=10, they also know the addition for the reverse of these first two numbers, that 6+4=10. It should also be pointed out that once students memorize *half* of the number facts, they already know the other half because they are just the reverse of the first half. For example: if 3+6=9, then they already know the number fact of 6+3=9. The same is true of the multiplication tables. Once students learn that 3×6=18, then they already know that 6×3=18. Pointing out the fact that students only need to memorize half of the chart and that they will automatically know the other half, makes the memorization of numbers facts much less overwhelming for students and reduces the time students need to spend on the memorization of facts.

Sample of Addition Number Chart:

1 +0 1	1 +1 2	1 +2 3	1 +3 4	1 +4 5	1 +5 6	1 +6 7	1 +7 8	1 +8 9	1 +9 10
2 +0 2	2 +1 3	2 +2 4	2 +3 5	2 +4 6	2 +5 7	2 +6 8	2 +7 9	2 +8 10	2 +9 11
3 +0 3	3 +1 4	3 +2 5	3 +3 6	3 +4 7	3 +5 8	3 +6 9	3 +7 10	3 +8 11	3 +9 12
4 +0 4	4 +1 5	4 +2 6	4 +3 7	4 +4 8	4 +5 9	4 +6 10	4 +7 11	4 +8 12	4 +9 13
5 +0 5	5 +1 6	5 +2 7	5 +3 8	5 +4 9	5 +5 10	5 +6 11	5 +7 12	5 +8 13	5 +9 14
6 +0 6	6 +1 7	6 +2 8	6 +3 9	6 +4 10	6 +5 11	6 +6 12	6 +7 13	6 +8 14	6 +9 15
7 +0 7	7 +1 8	7 +2 9	7 +3 10	7 +4 11	7 +5 12	7 +6 13	7 +7 14	7 +8 15	7 +9 16
8 +0 8	8 +1 9	8 +2 10	8 +3 11	8 +4 12	8 +5 13	8 +6 14	8 +7 15	8 +8 16	8 +9 17
9 +0 9	9 +1 10	9 +2 11	9 +3 12	9 +4 13	9 +5 14	9 +6 15	9 +7 16	9 +8 17	9 +9 18

It is essential to concentrate on the basic concept of the tens. Since so much of mathematics is based on tens, helping students to internalize this concept makes learning mathematics facts easier to accomplish. Using visual aids such as beads, sticks, and pennies, students should work with the groupings of 1+9, 2+8, 3+7, 4+6 and 5+5. Once they begin to internalize the concept of the groupings of basic tens, work should begin on memorization of the facts that equal ten. It should be pointed out that if students learn that 1+9 equals 10, the first two digits can be reversed (9+1=10) and the results are the same. The basic number facts that add up to ten should be placed on flashcards for students to memorize. Repeated review of the ten number facts is essential so that this concept becomes instilled in the minds of students and they have a good feeling for the pattern of these numbers. It is an essential concept for all students to master. For once students understand this concept, mathematical number patterns make more sense, and as a result, students find it easier, for example, to add columns of numbers quickly and accurately.

Students can learn the addition of numbers that are added to nine in one lesson if they are taught the "The Secret of the Nines." This involves demonstrating and teaching the fact that nine takes one away from the number being added to make a ten. Therefore, if you are adding nine to the numbers one through nine and you take one away from the number to be added, and then add a one in front of the result, you quickly have the correct answer. For example 9+1 (take 1 from 1 and it is 0) so 9+1=a 0 with a 1 in front of it, which is 10. 9+2 (Take 1 from 2 and it is 1) so 9+2=1 with a 1 in front of it, which is 11. And 9+4=13 (3 is one *less* than 4). Students seem to find it to be an easy, understandable and enjoyable way to master the art of fact memorization of the nines.

When teachers begin to work with subtracting nine from any number in the teens, they can teach students that the "Secret of the Nines," when subtracting from teens, is that the answer is one *more* than the teen ones column number. So 14–9=5 (5 is 1 more than the four in the teen one's column) so the answer is 5. 13–9=4 (the answer of 4 is one more than the 3), 17–9=8 (the answer of 8 is one more than the 7 in the teen one's column).

Once students begin to understand fact concepts and memorize number facts, those facts should be included in mathematical exercises on a consistent basis for added reinforcement. Music and rhymes can also sometimes be useful in reinforcing number fact memorization. There are CD and DVD recordings that teach number facts through the reciting of rhymes or the singing of songs. However, they often present too many facts at one time, thereby proving to be too much for students to grasp at any one time. While CD and DVD recordings can be effective if students are eager to listen to them multiple times, learning disabled students often find them overwhelming and end up learning very few fact rhymes or songs. A more effective way to teach students facts using rhymes or songs is for the educator to teach only two or three number facts during each lesson, reviewing the old facts before introducing the new ones. Some examples of number fact rhymes are:

6 times 6 is 36. Watch me while I pick up sticks.

9 times 9 is 81. With this you can have some fun.

6 times 4 is 24. Now you have them on the floor.

Rhymes and songs should be recited or sung consistently and repeatedly for long term memory development.

When teaching basic mathematical functions, any "tricks" that can be taught to students will aid in their ability to learn the functions faster and to develop their confidence in being able to handle new skills in mathematics. For example, when teaching children to subtract from a number that has a long row of zeros, such as:

90005
-21146

Think: *8999 (15)*

~~90005~~

- <u>21146</u>

Think: "When the bottom number in the ones column is bigger than the top number, I go next door to borrow one ten. I add that ten to the number in the ones column. However, whenever I go next door and borrow from zeros, they become nines. When I reach the number to the left of the zeros, I take one away from that number." Thus in this example, the five becomes fifteen, the zeros all become nines and the nine becomes an eight. It works every time, and makes subtracting from zeros easy for students to learn.

It is also important to teach students to learn to examine their calculation work carefully as they work, and to be certain that they have paid attention to the mathematical signs. Educators should frequently remind students, especially learning disabled students, to look carefully at the signs before they begin their calculations until it becomes automatic for them to do so. Students must be geared toward thinking, "Is there a minus sign which means to subtract or an addition sign which means to add?" In addition, it is not uncommon for learning disabled students to learn how to calculate one type of mathematical process and then, when another type is taught, for the student to forget the first process. For example, after students seem to have a good understanding of addition of a two digit number to a two digit number and the teacher goes on to teach subtraction of a two digit number from a two digit number, learning disabled students may be able to make a switch in their minds to the subtraction, but forget the addition. To insure that there is no memory loss, it is essential for educators to include one or two problems with addition, mixed with problems with subtraction. Initially, some students may not note the difference and subtract all of the problems. However, if students are reminded to look for the plus or minus sign, and are faced with work that requires changing from subtraction to addition, they will learn to master both skills and learn how to change their thinking from one process to another with ease. Likewise, if the teacher is teaching multiplication and then goes on to the teaching of division, exercises that include both multiplication and division should be given to students to help them learn to switch their mode of thinking and handle both processes.

When teaching fractions there are many "tricks" that can be taught to help students learn the process quickly and easily. For instance, when students are faced with unlike denominators, to cut down on the frustration that students, especially learning disabled students, feel when trying to determine the correct common denominator, educators should suggest that students begin by trying the highest denominator number for the common denominator as presented in the following problem:

For example: $\dfrac{3}{4}$ 12

$\dfrac{6}{12}$ 12

+ $\dfrac{2}{3}$ 12

A common denominator using the largest number, 12, would work in the above example. This happens frequently with the addition or subtraction of fractions. However, if it does not work, it is helpful to teach students to take the largest denominator number and multiply it by two to see if it would work as a common denominator that can be divided equally by each denominator.

For example: 9x2=18 and 18 can be divided equally by the denominators 6 and 3, so 18 is the common denominator for the following problem:

$\dfrac{5}{6}$ 18

$\dfrac{4}{9}$ 18

+ $\dfrac{2}{3}$ 18

If multiplying the largest denominator by two does not work, students should be taught to try multiplying by three, four and five until they come to the number that can be used as a common denominator and divided equally by all given denominators.

Recently, many schools in the United States have adopted a mathematics program entitled, *Everyday Mathematics,* designed at the University of Chicago as a result of a school mathematics project. This program is the result of twenty-five years of research and is designed to give children a better understanding of mathematical concepts and how they work. It has been my experience, however, that while this program works well for some children, it is very difficult for others to comprehend and master, especially learning disabled students. One of the main reasons is that students are asked to use more steps for the computation of basic mathematic skills. These added steps make the process to be learned more complicated and less comprehensible for students who struggle with mathematics.

Sample of *Everyday Mathematics* multiplication versus the standard method:

Everyday Mathematics Method			Standard Method
	100 10s 1s		
	2 6		2 6
	* 4 2		x 4 2
40* 20	8 0 0	step 1	5 2
40* 6	2 4 0	step 2	1040
2* 20	4 0	step 3	1,092
2* 6	1 2	step 4	
	1, 0 9 2	step 5	

Sample of *Everyday Mathematics* division versus the standard method:

Everyday Mathematics Method	Standard Method

$$1,010/6= ?$$

$$
\begin{array}{r}
168 \\
6\overline{)1,010} \\
-\;6 \\
\hline
4\,1 \\
-\,36 \\
\hline
5\,0 \\
-\,48 \\
\hline
2
\end{array}
$$

Everyday Mathematics Method:

$$
\begin{array}{rc}
6\overline{)1,010} & \\
-600 & 100 \\
\hline
410 & \\
\\
-300 & 50 \\
\hline
110 & \\
\\
-\;60 & 10 \\
\hline
50 & \\
\\
-48 & \;\;8 \\
\hline
2 & 168
\end{array}
$$

The answer is 168 with a remainder of 2.

With both the multiplication and division, the standard method is more compact, done with fewer steps, and takes less time, paper space and student effort than the *Everyday Mathematics* method. Students who find mathematics difficult learn better when a less challenging, more simplified mathematical process is taught to them. They respond better to traditional mathematics and learn it with greater ease.

An educational trend that has recently been instituted in many school mathematics curriculums is to give calculators to students in elementary and middle schools for the calculation of basic mathematics computation. The reason given for this trend is that students must learn to use calculators. This means that in our schools we now have first graders using calculators, thus eliminating the "need" in school to memorize facts, learn to compute mentally, and to truly understand mathematical processes. This is a serious mistake.

Every second the human brain receives and processes approximately 72 gigabytes of visual information. The average brain can hold about 100 million megabytes of memory while modern computers provide only a few million megabytes of memory. It is a fact that our brains can hold far more information than the greatest computer ever made.

When we give students calculators, we are allowing students to slow down the development of their brain processing skills and their ability to memorize. In essence, we are handing them a crutch instead of teaching them how to exercise their brains to the fullest. Do we, as adults, walk around all day with a calculator in our pockets, pulling it out to perform simple mathematical calculations? When a child is, for example, at the community swimming pool and decides that he would like to buy a snack with his money, do we want him to have to bring a calculator with him to determine the cost of the items he wants to buy? I certainly hope not! Students must be required to memorize mathematical facts and processes so that they can use this knowledge on a daily basis without having to carry around an electronic device, when their brain is an intricate and magnificent electronic device, and is something that they carry with them at all times. If educators feel that students need to learn how to use calculators, one chapter in the mathematics textbook could be included for the teaching of this skill beginning in grade four. But to include calculators in the daily mathematics curriculum beginning in first grade is to short change our students by limiting their growth, development, thinking and reasoning skills in mathematics. Therefore, we need to limit the use of calculators at the elementary and middle school levels.

WORD PROBLEM SOLVING

Our ultimate goal in the teaching of mathematics is for students to be able to solve mathematical problems that they face or will face during their lifetime on a daily basis. Therefore, mathematical word problem solving needs to be presented in such a way that students truly understand the tremendous value that mathematic processes and problem solving exercises offer them. Each chapter in the mathematics text should include word problems. These word problems should pertain to practical everyday experiences that children have that involve a need to solve a mathematics problem. They might be built around problems that need to be solved when playing popular board games, shopping for toys or school supplies, or daily routine activities. Children should be encouraged to write their own word problems and then solve them. A class booklet of word problems created by the students, and monitored carefully by the teacher so that the word problems are correctly and clearly stated, would be an excellent way to instill interest and understanding of word problem solving that occurs every day in their lives.

A common problem facing learning disabled students who experience difficulty with word problem solving is their inability to read the word problem. This is often due to the fact that they have not learned to read vocabulary that is related to mathematics. For this reason, it is essential for educators and parents to work with students on the reading of word problems and common mathematical terms such as *addition, subtraction, multiplication, division, product, quotient, equals, minus, rectangular, triangle, percent, fraction, distance, proportion, and decimal*. Beginning readers need to learn to read simple terms that are frequently used in mathematical word problems such as *greater than, less than, altogether, total number, how many, change, spent, total amount, spend*, and *solve*. As students progress in school, they need to learn to read more advanced terms such as *rectangle, estimate, height, approximately, compute, equation, perimeter, dimension, combined weight, line segment, compatible number*, and *equivalent*.

When educators initially begin working with students on simple addition and subtraction word problems, it is also very helpful to teach key words or phrases that give them a *clue* as to what process to use to solve the word problem. It is not uncommon to find students who think that a word problem that has the words, "How many *more*…?" think that "more" means to add. For this reason, educators should teach students that word problems containing the words, "How many *more*…?" or, "How many *less*…?" actually are clues to *subtract*. They should also teach students that with word problems that ask, "How many *in all?*" or, "How many are there *altogether?*" the correct function is to *add*. When studying multiplication, it is important to teach students that when the word problem asks the student to find the *product*, you must *multiply,* and when the word problem asks the student to find the *quotient*, you must *divide*. When students recognize clue words found in word problems and understand how they are to be used, it helps them to feel more confident and less intimidated about solving mathematical word problems. As a result, they feel more relaxed and are much more eager to solve word problems. This, in turn, makes mathematics less frustrating and more enjoyable for them.

Another helpful technique with word problem solving, especially for learning disabled students, is to have the students draw simple pictures that demonstrate the word problem. This helps them to comprehend better exactly what the word problem is asking and how they can solve the problem.

For example:

Uncle John flew 370 miles on Tuesday and 150 miles on Thursday. How much farther did he fly on Tuesday than Thursday?

Tuesday _____ 370 miles

Thursday _____ 150 miles

Or:

Maria has 3 cats. Her friend Megan has 2 dogs and 1 parrot. How many pets do they have all together?

Maria's pets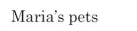

Megan's pets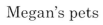

Pictures help students visualize word problems, to see how the process they use affects the results, and to visually understand that the answers to the word problems must make sense.

A third very effective technique in the teaching of word problems is to teach students how to design and write their own word problems. Educators should begin by demonstrating the process of developing a word problem based on a mathematical process that has been taught to the students. The component parts should be discussed, and the word problem process and solution shown, with stress being placed on a solution that makes sense. Students should then follow their educator's pattern, and design a word problem of their own that is pertinent to a need that they might have for using the same mathematical process. Once students begin to feel comfortable designing and solving their own word problems, they should then be instructed to create word problems for their classmates to solve. After their word problems are designed, they need to solve the word problems themselves on a separate piece of paper before passing them on to their classmates so that they know the correct answers to their own problems. This can be an exciting as well as a great learning experience for students. Lastly, this technique lends itself beautifully to the creation of two step word problems.

For example, the word problem might be:

> Jack bought a baseball cap for $4.50 and a baseball tee shirt for $8.95. He gave the shop owner $15.00. How much change did he receive?

> Step One:

> Students must understand that first they need to add the cost of the cap and tee shirt to find the total cost of the items.

$$\begin{array}{r} \$4.50 \\ + 8.95 \\ \hline \$13.45 \text{ total cost of items} \end{array}$$

Step Two:

The total cost must be subtracted from the
amount of money given to the shop owner
to determine the change he received.

$15.00 money given to shop owner
-13.45 total cost of items
$ 1.55 change received

This type of word problem solving teaching technique
should be used with each new mathematical function
taught throughout elementary and middle school. By
having students design their own word problems, word
problem solving becomes more personal and thus more
comprehensible for students, providing them with a
true eagerness to solve word problems.

In summary, much can be done to help learning
disabled students who experience serious problems
with mathematics to help them overcome their difficulties. Stress must be placed initially on developing
the learning skills of visual and auditory perception
and, in particular, visual and auditory memory. When
learning skill development is coupled with a concentrated program that is developmentally presented and
based on a traditional mathematical teaching approach, one that includes the teaching of "tricks" to
make mathematics learning easier, consistent reinforcement and review, learning disabled students make
great gains in mathematics. As students overcome their
weaknesses, they begin to feel confident, and to enjoy
and apply mathematics to their daily lives.

CHAPTER 11

THE RIGHT READING APPROACH

For years educators have debated about the right reading approach for all children. In the early 1900's the approach and emphasis was on phonics. While most children could spell and sound out words easily with this approach, educators found that some children were not reading fluently because they had to take time to sound out many words as they read. The *phonetic* approach to reading was criticized for putting too much emphasis on breaking up words into common word parts and syllables, and too little on memorization of words. A change was made to a pure *sight* approach, a *whole word* approach. The vocabulary taught to students was presented developmentally and controlled by the textbook designers. Once a word was introduced *that* word would be found again and again throughout the reading textbook and matching workbook. The use of phonics was nearly eliminated. Children were taught by means of flashcards to memorize words relying on whole word learning. The positive result was that these children could read more fluently than the phonetically taught students. The downfall of this method was that most children could not decipher unknown words on their own. In addition, if children had a difficult time visually recalling the appearance of a word when writing, they were not able to rely on phonetic knowledge to spell it.

When the sight approach did not seem to be working, educators shifted back to a phonetic approach called *Initial Teaching Alphabet* (ITA) which had children reading words that were printed with phonetic symbols. For example, the letters *o* and *e* would be connected to symbolize the long *o* sound in a word like *poem.* Words in the primary basal readers were written phonetically even though some of the words were not spelled correctly. For example, *yesterday* would be spelled as *yesterdae, building* as *bilding,* and *cold* as *coeld.* One of the problems with this technique was that children often had a difficult time switching from the phonetically misspelled words to reading or writing words that were spelled correctly. Also, some children relied heavily on the phonetic symbols, and eliminating them later in the program left the students without the ability to sound out words.

When the *ITA* approach failed, educators decided to try a *linguistic* method which was a whole word approach that stressed reading for meaning and the belief that the acquisition of language competence comes from listening, reading, speaking and writing. The listening aspect of the program primarily involved listening to others read; the speaking involved oral reading expression. Suggestions for optional independent activities that included written expression were provided for the teacher. Most of the textbooks included stories, poems and plays, with black and white or colored illustrations. However, most of the illustrations were not appealing and the clarity of the illustrations was poor. Realizing that reading should not be an isolated subject but, rather, involved in the learning of all subjects, educators began to stress the importance of including stories related to science and history into basal readers. Most readers had a glossary, and some instruction in word meaning was included in the program. The linguistic reading program was a positive step forward in that it did help children realize that reading is not only about reading fiction, but informative material as well. A readability analysis was done on the literature to determine grade appropriateness. However, most of the reading programs did not have a controlled vocabulary for primary readers. Words were taught in word families, called *phonograms*, or on the basis of similar patterns, but only as whole words. For example, learning the phonogram *at* would lead to learning *cat, fat, pat,* and *flat*. Most of the readers lacked step by step developmental phonetic instruction. Educators were discouraged from breaking words down into their component parts.

Incorporated into the linguistic readers, along with the science and history related stories, was some work in study and reference skills. Worksheets became very popular at that time. Teachers were often free to select and use worksheets to their liking. Although a grade level was assigned to the worksheets by the publisher, because the vocabulary within the worksheets was not correlated to the reading textbook, it required students to read many words to which they had never been exposed. As a result, many students experienced difficulty reading the worksheets.

Because the linguistic reading approach leaned heavily on reading for meaning, the *cloze* procedure became very popular in the classrooms. This is a teaching technique that involves asking students to fill in the word or phrase that makes sense in the sentence or paragraph. For example:

The rabbit _____ the clover.

ran, sniffed, guess, hopped

The problem with using this technique was that students, especially those in the upper grades where paragraphs were used, could guess the missing word by reading *only* the words around the blank. As a result, these students often were able to accurately fill in the blank without even reading the whole paragraph or story. It became a game for some students who marked answers quickly with little concern about reading the whole passage.

At the same time educators started to stress the teaching of specific comprehension skills such as understanding what is inferred, remembering details, drawing conclusions, understanding the use of antecedents, comparison and contrast. This was good, until it was carried to extremes. Entire workbooks were designed to teach each skill separately. For example, all of the exercises in one workbook would involve drawing conclusions. When each skill was presented in isolation, students began to figure out patterns for answering questions in a workbook without truly grasping the comprehension of the passage or understanding the skill. Consequently, when that same skill was presented in a workbook that was mixed with other types of comprehension skills, and students were not able to rely on a similar pattern, they frequently were unable to identify the process required to answer the question correctly.

When educators decided that the linguistic approach, as it was presented at that time, was not effective enough, they began looking for another "innovative" approach to reading. Many educators felt that most basal readers were not appealing to students. They wanted reading material that would do a better job of heightening students' interest in reading. Educators in Australia had developed a new program that they felt was successful with their students. It was called the *whole language* approach to reading. *Crocodile Dundee,* a film about an Australian, had just been released in America, and it initiated a keen interest in the country. When American educators heard about the excitement of the Australian teachers with their new reading program, they began to examine the program and to think that perhaps the Australian teachers had the answer. America needed a reading program that would be more appealing to children. So, we adopted the Australian whole language method.

The whole language method of teaching reading stems from the idea that language based on good literature connects us to everyday life. The program evolved from the linguistic approach. The whole language program, which is still in use in some schools today, consists of large, beautifully illustrated books for the teacher and small matching books for the students. The teacher puts the big book on an easel and reads the story aloud to the children while pointing to each word. Then, the same story is read again, but this time the children read along with the teacher in unison, called *choral reading.* Choral reading is usually repeated.

Then the children are asked to read their own book, the same book in a smaller size. There is little or no control by the textbook designers for the developmental presentation of vocabulary. The interest level of the material and general difficulty level of the vocabulary for each grade largely determines the selection of the material for each grade. Without books with controlled vocabulary, hundreds of words are presented to first graders and, somehow, all children are expected to be able to quickly make them a part of their sight vocabulary. Many children are totally overwhelmed by the amount of vocabulary they are expected to learn simply by hearing a story read over and over again. Workbooks and worksheets are non-existent in this program. Teachers are often left to decide on their own whether or not supplementary materials will be used in their classroom. In addition, formal instruction of phonics is not a part of the whole language approach. Realizing that children simply cannot decipher words independently without phonics, some teachers have either designed their own worksheets or used old phonics workbooks to teach their students phonics. The assumption that all children will learn to read well if they are simply presented with beautifully illustrated, highly interesting books that are read to them over and over again, is proving to be untrue.

Educators are beginning to realize that the whole language approach is not meeting the needs of all students. Whole language assumes that children will assimilate word knowledge simply by listening to words read as they view them and that children will, through the process of inference, figure out phonics on their own. This is simply not happening for many children. As a result, programmers from New Zealand devised what they call, the *Reading Recovery* program. This is a program designed for children who are being taught with the whole language approach and need remedial work. It is meant to be a short-term process that has children reading familiar stories while the teacher, using shorthand miscue recording techniques, notes the types of errors made by the children. No formal remediation is incorporated to teach children phonetic skills that they need to know to correct their errors. The teacher encourages self-correction by use of cues such as language syntax or visual formation of print. More opportunities are offered for the children to read and write, using some letter-sound relationship identification. While some reading improvement has been evident with this remedial approach, this procedure fails to meet the needs of remedial students with its absence of a basic developmental approach that includes a solid program of phonics as well as other basic reading skills.

In recent years, we have seen some of our school districts employ an *integrated reading* and *language arts* approach to reading, which incorporates the linguistic and whole language philosophy. It is a literature based reading program, with supplemental workbooks, that integrates reading instruction with vocabulary, comprehension, and language arts exercises such as speaking, writing, spelling and grammar. While the textbook designers state that the teaching of listening skills is included in their programs, the listening exercises involve practice in listening, not developmentally presented exercises to teach listening skills. The recognition by educators and textbook designers of the importance of integrating language arts with all core subjects *is* a positive step forward, for reading and writing do go hand in hand and children need to understand the use of written expression as it relates to all subjects. While this approach has merit in terms of written expression, the textbooks do not include a step by step developmental approach for the teaching of writing, one that encompasses all styles of writing. While a general readability level has been assigned to the textbooks, we still have basal readers that lack controlled vocabulary at the primary level, a complete developmental approach to phonics, and most importantly, developmental instruction of visual and auditory memory and perception, thinking, work and study skills areas.

In 1994 the Department of Education reported that forty percent of all fourth graders in the United States were reading below the basic reading level. As a result of serious concern by educators and parents about the inadequate reading levels of our students, a *National Reading Panel* was formed. In April of 2000, the National Reading Panel published a researched-based report of what constitutes a good reading program. It was entitled, *Teaching Children to Read*. It presented their findings on the effectiveness of various teaching methods which included alphabetics (phonemic awareness and phonics instruction), fluency, comprehension (vocabulary and text comprehension) and teacher training. While the value of using computers to teach reading was evaluated, the final result of this research was not definite, with an admission by the panel that more research should be done in this area. Then, in September of 2001, the panel wrote a second document based on their research, entitled *Put Reading First*. They determined that there are five essential elements that good readers need in order to master the art of reading. They are phonetic awareness, phonics, fluency, vocabulary, and text comprehension. Their recommendation was for educators to base their reading programs on this Scientifically Based Reading Research (SBRR).

As a result of the findings of the panel, the United States government adopted the *No Child Left Behind Act* in 2001 and set it into action the following year. The goal of this act is that by the year 2014 and beyond, all children in the United States will be proficient in reading.

So far, the results of this new SBRR approach have proved promising. Publishing companies are beginning to develop programs based on these findings. Improvements have been noted in reading scores, particularly for fifth graders. As a result of this enactment and the discrediting of elements of the whole language approach, structured phonics and controlled vocabulary have re-entered the scene. While most current reading programs are not strictly based on the whole language approach to reading, elements of the whole language approach still remain within the programs.

For years we have switched our emphasis from one reading approach to another. Unfortunately, in the past our attempts with "innovative" programs have not solved our reading problems. It is refreshing to know that these recommendations are based on the SBRR program and that some progress is beginning to be made.

There is much to be done, however. The *National*

Council on Learning Disabilities reported that 2.7 million public school students nationwide in 2007 had been identified as learning disabled. In 2009, the *Alliance for Excellent Education* reported that 1.2 million students in the United States were high school dropouts. In some inner city public schools, the dropout rate is as high as fifty percent with twenty-five percent of these students classified as learning disabled. Yet, we have the know-how to drastically lower this figure. The National Reading Panel has stated that the solution lies in the *way* that we implement what we already have, and *what* is included in our programs. Certainly, this *is* a key factor.

A number of years ago I assembled, out of necessity, a reading program for my students. It was successful for all children, learning disabled as well as children who were not learning disabled. It quickly expanded the reading skills of students who were poor readers as well as students who were functioning well in a gifted program. It met the needs of all students who innately had average to above average potential. How was my program different? It was based on an eclectic approach, a combined approach that covered every avenue of learning and encompassed much more than phonics, vocabulary and comprehension. Since at that time an eclectic reading program had never been produced, in order to create this type of a program materials were selected from many different sources. A basal reading series that offered a controlled vocabulary was used for the primary grade level students, while a readability-controlled linguistic series was selected for the upper grade level students. The best exercises from various publishing company workbooks were chosen to teach a structured program of phonics, syllabication, comprehension, writing, thinking, and study skills. Most importantly, teaching materials to develop *all* of the learning skills of visual perception, visual memory, auditory perception, and auditory memory were utilized. As a result, remedial students learned to read at grade level, and in most cases, well above grade level. Learning disabled students erased their deficiencies and began to learn in their classrooms with confidence and ease. All of the other students, average to gifted, flourished.

If we were to institute in our schools a solid program based on an eclectic approach, one that would include it all, we would solve our reading problems. Should we include phonics in our reading program? Absolutely! Without a good understanding of phonics children cannot sound out unknown words independently. Since seventy-five percent of all words can be phonetically decoded for reading and spelling, we should not deprive our students of this valuable skill. It is refreshing to know that educational publishers have begun to design new reading programs that incorporate the formal instruction of phonics. They are beginning, also, to make some needed changes in the order in which we teach phonics.

In the past, phonetic programs included the teaching of all of the consonants *before* the teaching of vowels. However, since all words in English have at least one vowel, once children know the most frequently used consonant sounds, they should be taught the vowels and the basic rules of vowel usage. The earlier children learn the letter sounds, vowels and vowel combinations, the earlier they can make the connection between let-ter-sound identification and sounding out words. What good is it for children to know the consonant sounds, if they have not been taught, as soon as possible, to un-derstand why they are learning them? By the time children reach fourth grade, they should have been taught *all* basic and advanced phonetic sounds, phono-grams, and most syllabication skills. They should have been taught, for example, that *ture* at the end of a word, sounds like *cher,* that *tion* sounds like *shun,* and the difference between the prefixes, *pre, pro,* and *per.* Most importantly, children need to know how to apply their knowledge of phonics to the sounding out of words. Therefore, stress should be placed on the application of phonics, and practice in the decoding of unknown words using their phonetic knowledge, structural analysis and blending skills. However, teaching children to read by using *solely* a phonetic approach is not, as we realize now, the solution to the reading problem.

Most students who are good readers have memo-rized thousands of words. When they read they simply know the words by sight and do not have to stop to sound out each word they come across. Should we in-clude a sight approach within our reading program? Yes! Nothing is more painful than to see a child "pho-netic bound," sounding out each word that he comes across painfully and slowly because he has a poor sight vocabulary and has not memorized words. So we must include the development of a solid sight vocabulary and sight vocabulary teaching techniques, such as flash-cards, in every reading program. Most importantly, particularly in grades one through three, this vocabu-lary must be controlled. Publishers must begin with easy one-syllable words, using the Dolch lists of the most commonly read words, and design their program so that once a word is introduced in the text it is used over and over again. Beginning readers learn through repetition of material that is presented gradually and developmentally. Vocabulary control is essential. We do not expect our students to read third year German, Spanish, Italian or French before they have been introduced to a basic first and second year vocabulary. Why then, do we bombard first graders with hundreds of words through the whole language approach or some of the newer modified reading programs, and expect them to memorize so many new words after hearing them a few times? We must provide then, basal readers with a highly controlled vocabulary, especially for the primary grades. In addition, there are readability formulas that can be used to determine the reading grade level of material based on the length of the sentences in the text and the number of syllables in words. Textbook designers must establish appropriate readability levels for all elementary textbooks, but especially for basal readers and their supplementary workbooks. At the same time, there is no reason why we cannot include beautifully illustrated, interesting stories and classic literature similar to what we see in the whole language books, but with controlled vocabulary. Included in the readers should be material related to science, history and literature, for it *is* important to prepare our students for the reading of all types of materials, not just fictional material.

Should there be a linguistic emphasis on reading for meaning in our program? Yes! Reading isn't really reading unless you understand what you have read.

The National Reading Panel's recommendation for a strong emphasis on reading comprehension must be heeded. However, students have to be able to mechanically read words before they can even begin to comprehend even simple sentences. In addition, being able to mechanically read words well is an essential foundation for learning advanced comprehension skills. How can children begin to understand, for example, what is inferred in a sentence, if they cannot mechanically read enough words to make sense out of it? Once there is a foundation upon which children can begin to expand their comprehension skills, all areas of comprehension including such skills as remembering details, understanding the main idea, comparison and contrast, inference, and reasoning and thinking skills should be taught.

Most importantly, the formal teaching of word meaning should not be ignored in reading programs. How can children read for meaning if they do not have a good understanding of the meaning of the words they are reading? It is easy to assume that because children can read a word, they know the meaning of the word. Yet, all too often, this is not the case. In addition, sometimes children believe that they know the meaning of a word but, if they are asked to define it, come up with a meaning that is not at all accurate. At my learning center teachers often recorded the humorous inaccurate definitions that their students gave them in defining a word. Some of the responses they recorded were: tusks, something on an elephant made out of soap; measles, tiny mice; hairdresser, place where you put things for your hair; rectory, where you go when you wreck your car; and prevailed, getting dressed before the wedding. We must not neglect the importance of asking children to define words to test them on their word meaning knowledge. Most importantly, formal instruction on this skill must be included throughout the entire reading program and incorporated in all subject areas.

Since reading and writing go hand in hand, the development of spelling and good written expression must be incorporated into the reading program as well as all core subjects such as social studies and science. Emphasis should be placed on good written expression as well as the mechanics of good penmanship, grammatical and technical writing skills. We must continue to include integrated language arts in our textbooks, but it must include all skills presented in a step by step developmental fashion, particularly at the elementary level. Detailed guidelines for teachers, suggested topics for essays and reports, and models of good writing should be included in the textbooks.

In addition, we need to use developmentally controlled workbooks that are correlated to the basal readers; workbooks that reinforce the skills that are being taught in basal readers. The workbooks should contain as much of the same vocabulary that is presented in the readers as possible, or at least the same level of vocabulary that is presented in the reader. These workbooks must include phonics and syllabication, with practice in sounding out words, sight vocabulary, word meaning, and all areas of comprehension, writing, thinking, work and study skills.

It is refreshing to note that, some educational publishers have started to produce beautifully illustrated, literature based, balanced reading programs that include all of the basic reading, spelling and writing skills with a more appropriately controlled reading level. While this is a major step forward, the skills that will bridge the gap between achievers and non-achievers and make the greatest impact on helping children with learning problems and lower the rate of high school dropouts, has not been fully addressed in these programs. Many children have not had the direction or academic stimulation during their preschool years that is needed to establish strong auditory and visual memory skills. These children often begin kindergarten with poor listening skills. When children are poor listeners, much of the instruction that goes on in the classroom is totally lost to them. If we do not include the specific instruction of listening skills, teaching them how to listen to isolated units of information as well as information presented in context, beginning in the primary grades, they will not be prepared to grasp basic reading and mathematical skills easily. Also, many underprivileged children also have not had the opportunity to develop their visual perception and visual memory skills. With underprivileged children these weaknesses often stem from not having had educational toys in their homes to help them develop these skills and from parents who have not had the time or the know-how to help their children to develop these skills because they are working two jobs or trying to raise a large family, often as a single parent. If educators do not develop the visual memory and visual perception of these children when they are in the primary grades, how can we expect them to visually recall enough of the material that we are teaching them in school to make it easy for them to achieve, and therefore, want to stay in school?

The most important addition that that we can make

to our primary curriculum today is the inclusion of the specific *teaching* of visual perception, visual memory, auditory perception, and auditory memory.

Is there a solution to *No Child Left Behind*? I know there is! The answer is to provide teachers with a balanced eclectic program, one that utilizes the best from *all* reading approaches and includes *all* skill areas, including learning, thinking and study skills. We are off to a good start with some new programs, such as the 2007 edition of *Reading Street,* a program of Scott Foresman. It is a good example of a solid effort on the part of the publisher to follow the National Reading Panel guidelines and offer a more balanced reading program. However, we still need a program that offers even greater vocabulary control, one that does not present an overwhelming amount of vocabulary in the primary grade levels, and a program that actually teaches visual and auditory memory and perception on a developmental basis. If this were to be done, we would find that there would be fewer children with learning disabilities, and more children who would be able to achieve success in school. For those who might still exhibit some learning skill weaknesses, special concentrated remedial instruction of these skills would be quick and easy. For with concentrated remediation that develops learning skills along with the basic reading, thinking, and study skills, learning disabilities *can* be cured.

Lastly, we need to revise our teacher training curriculums to include specific instruction on how best to teach all of the basic skills as well as learning, thinking and study skills. Publishing companies must be encouraged to include learning skills in their basal readers and workbooks, and more thinking and study skills in all textbooks. It is a task that will take time, but one that will prove to be tremendously rewarding for educators and students.

There is an answer to *No Child Left Behind.* It involves an approach that works for all children, one that helps them to reach their fullest potential. We have the ability and know-how to design and implement the perfect reading program, and to raise the level of literacy in the United States to an all time high. The National Reading Panel has helped us to get started. Now let's fill in the gaps and create a complete program, one that touches upon all of the skills needed to help *all* children, especially those with learning disabilities.

REFERENCES AND INDEX

REFERENCES

Bangs, Tina E. *Language and Learning Disorders of the Pro-Academic Child.* New York. Meredith Corporation, 1968.

Boning, Richard A. *Multiple Skills Series.* Ohio. Barnell Loft, SRA/McGraw Hill, 1998.

Cusimano, Addie. *Achieve: A Visual Memory Program.* Pennsylvania. Achieve Publications, 1980, 2003.

Cusimano, Addie. *Visual Discrimination: Noting Differences in Frequently Misperceived Words.* Pennsylvania. Achieve Publications, 2007.

Cusimano, Addie. *Auditory Sequential Memory Instructional Workbook.* Pennsylvania. Achieve Publications, 2005.

Dolch, Edward William. *Problems in Reading.* The Garrard Press, 1948.

Farrald, Robert R., and Richard G.Shamber. *A Diagnostic and Prescriptive Technique: A Mainstream Approach to Identification, Assessment and Amelioration of Learning Disabilities.* South Dakota. Adapt Press, 1973.

Frierson, Edward C., and Walter B. Barbe. *Educating Children with Learning Disabilities.* New York. Meredith Corporation, 1967.

Hittleman, Daniel R. *Developmental Reading: A Psycholinguistic Perspective.* Chicago. Rand McNally College Publishing Company, 1978.

Kratoville, Betty Lou. *Listen My Children and You Shall Hear.* Texas. Pro-Ed, 1987.

Lerner, Janet W. *Children with Learning Disabilities.* Massachusetts. Houghton Mifflin Company, 1971.

Mazurkiewicz, Albert J., and Harold J.Tanyzer. *Initial Teaching Alphabet.* New York. Initial Teaching Alphabet Publications, Inc., 1966.

National Academy of Sciences. *Mapping the Brain and its Functions.* Washington, DC. National Academy Press, 1991.

National Assessment of Educational Progress. *Nations Report Card.* http://nationsreportcard.gov/reading.

Scott Foresman Authors. *Reading Street.* New Jersey. Pearson Education, Inc., 2007.

Seiderman, Dr. Arthur S. and Dr. Steven E. Marcus. *20/20 is Not Enough.* New York. Alfred A. Knopf, Inc., 1989.

Wehrli, Kitty. *Symbol Discrimination and Sequencing.* California. Ann Arbor Publishers, Inc., a Division of Academic Therapy Publications, 1976.

Wehrli, Kitty. *Thought Tracking.* California. Ann Arbor Publishers, Inc., a Division of Academic Therapy Publications, 1976.

INDEX

imagination, 29,74
immaturity, 34,35
integrated language arts, 160
internalize, 18,19,31,34,97,101,119,126-128,131
IQ, 1,5,9,25,31,33,35,36,81,83-86
ITA, 147

kindergarten, 13,14,35,42,69,87,97,161

learning disabled, 1-9,14,16,22,24,25,28,31,33,35,
38,48,51,80,81,83,93,94,98,102,105,110,111-120,
122-125,127-129,133-135,137,141,142,145,155,156
learning modalities, 103
learning skill deficiencies, 1,3,5,6,8,9,35,83
learning skills, 1,3-5,9,35,53,85,97,98,112,122,145
156,162
left-handed students, 66
linear, 118
linguistic approach, 150
Listen My Children and You Shall Hear, 58
listening skills, 55,58,59
long term memory, 97,102,108,129-133

mathematical symbols, 113
mathematics, 111-145
meaningful categories, 105
measurement, 114,118-122
memorization, 108,111,122-124,128,130-133,146
mental computation, 113,114,125
metrics, 118,119,122
Michener, James, 27,70
misspelled, 31,32,147